Keep Your BONSAI *Perfectly Shaped*

Herb L. Gustafson

Sterling Publishing Co., Inc.
New York

ACKNOWLEDGMENTS

I would like to recognize the contribution made by my students. Their constant questions and challenging bonsai projects help me focus on the need for this book. Thanks go to those who have allowed me to photograph their projects to help others learn.

I appreciate the efforts of Sheri Zet- tel on the transcription and word processing of this manuscript. You did an excellent job in a timely fashion with an unfamiliar subject. My father, as always, has provided me with his stable and unjudgmental affection, and for that I remain grateful.

Photographs by the author

Drawings by Lynn Boyd

Designed by Judy Morgan

Library of Congress Cataloging-in-Publication Data
Gustafson, Herb L.
    Keep your bonsai perfectly shaped   /   Herb L. Gustafson.
        p.   cm.
    Includes index.
    ISBN 0-8069-8134-2
    1. Bonsai. I. Title.
SB433.5.G8735   1996
635.9'772—dc20   96-35804
                                                                              CIP

1   3   5   7   9   10   8   6   4   2

Published by Sterling Publishing Company, Inc.
387 Park Avenue South, New York, N.Y. 10016
© 1997 by Herb L. Gustafson
Distributed in Canada by Sterling Publishing
% Canadian Manda Group, One Atlantic Avenue, Suite 105
Toronto, Ontario, Canada M6K 3E7
Distributed in Great Britain and Europe by Cassell PLC
Wellington House, 125 Strand, London WC2R 0BB, England
Distributed in Australia by Capricorn Link (Australia) Pty Ltd.
P.O. Box 6651, Baulkham Hills, Business Centre, NSW 2153, Australia
Printed in Hong Kong
All right reserved

Sterling ISBN 0-8069-8134-2

INTRODUCTION

I often hear, "This bonsai doesn't look quite right," or "I am not happy with my tree," or even, "Is this bonsai salvageable?" In bonsai we do indeed have a guide, and it is right before us. All too often we forget the lessons that nature has taught us. Indeed, the original bonsai was a tree that had been shaped by nature's forces. We appreciate bonsai as potted trees, yet we soon forget their source of inspiration. With nature as our blueprint, we can return to the very roots of this art form and style our trees with confidence. Our newfound assurance and heightened awareness can restore relaxation, enjoyment, and enthusiasm to an art often encumbered by rules. The Buddhist monk 1000 years ago who meditated over his collected bonsai was experiencing the same emotions we experience today. Connect with that history. Learn from nature, and keep your bonsai perfectly shaped; do it for the personal satisfaction it gives you.

THE FORMAL UPRIGHT STYLE

Shokkan

Fig. 1-1.

THE FIVE INCLINATIONS OF THE TRUNK

The Three Upright Styles

The **formal upright style** is perhaps the most common style of tree that we find in nature. As a new tree develops from seed it reaches upward toward the light. The trunk grows straight and tall. **Fig. 1-1** shows many trees of different sizes and ages, yet a uniform serenity surrounds all of them because of their straight trunks. Young trees are growing below older trees in a calm setting that gives us a feeling of repose. Even cartoon trees or stick figure trees are drawn with a straight trunk and branches in a triangular shape at the top of the trunk. It is a design that we see often; it is something we feel comfortable with; and it is the shape that we see most often in nature.

Obviously not all trees are straight and tall. Due to adverse conditions such as rain, wind, snow, or drought, sometimes a tree is forced to incline slightly to one side or another. As it tries to grow vertically, the trunk forms a slight bend. Trees that have a slight bend are known in the bonsai

world as **informal upright** trees. A tree that has an inclination to one side and yet recovers so that the top of the tree is still over the base of the trunk suggests the presence of environmental

Fig. 1-2. **This Scotch pine, pinus sylvestris,** *displays an upright trunk line and a distinct foliage triangle.*

Fig. 1-3. **A slanting-style Scotch pine, pinus sylvestris,** *illustrating the importance of strong lower branches and defined apex.*

stress. Some type of stress or adversity caused the tree to lean slightly over to one side, and yet the tree still recovers. Refer to chapter 2.

Yet another style of tree seen in nature is the **slanting style**. In the woods many trees have been slightly uprooted or slightly blown over by wind or snow and are unable to recover. Slanting trees point toward the light, away from shadows of larger trees around them. Slanting trees lean out over water, and sometimes they try to grow from the side of a mountain. It is difficult for these trees to recover because of the

adverse conditions under which they grow. The slanting style suggests a bit more stress, therefore, than the previous two styles mentioned. Refer to chapter 3.

The Cascading Styles

The **semi-cascade style** is found in even more extreme environments. The semi-cascade style started as an upright style, but the lowest branch begins to extend itself out and below the trunk. Harsh environmental conditions are usually found on the tops of

Fig. 1-4.

Fig. 1-5. A grouping of formal upright cypress, **chamaecyparis thyoides andelyensis** *'conica'. Part of a* **saikei** *planting.*

mountains, in gorges or around rocky ledges. Whenever it is easier for lower branches to grow faster than upper ones, the semi-cascade style prevails. Refer to chapter 4.

The **cascade style** is the furthest extreme of the five inclinations of the trunk. In the cascading style, the entire length of trunk tries to recover from the stress that it feels in the environment, but the lower branches are far more successful than the branches at the top of the tree. We see extreme cascading style trees on the edges of rocky ravines, gorges, and high desert ledges. The lowest branch on a cascading tree is the strongest grower. It is the longest branch, often extending far below the root buttress of the tree. These make spectacular trees to view, and are frequently photographed and copied in bonsai. Refer to chapter 5.

STYLE CONSIDERATIONS

The Inclination of the Trunk

Bonsai imitates nature, so try to learn from trees that are growing naturally. To display a bonsai as an unstressed plant, the formal upright style is usually a good choice. On the other hand, to convey wind or other environmental stress on a plant the formal upright style is usually not the way to go, because the formal upright style gives the viewer a sense of calm, a sense that the tree's environment is constant and never changing. **Fig. 1-6** shows a tree that, despite a high altitude, wind, and intense light, still grows upward. Its branches may be battered, its roots may be exposed, and it may have some

Fig. 1-6.

dead wood on it, but in general, it grows upright, without resistance from the sides. The stresses it feels are not so forceful as to have caused the trunk to lean toward one side or another. The trunk grows straight up. In designing bonsai, keep in mind that certain trees look best without swaying branches and without an angle to the trunk. This is the formal upright style.

Some formal upright trees are short, others are tall. Some display their branches wide to the sides, others have branches only on one side and not the other. The one thing all formal upright trees have in common is the straightness of the trunk. Sometimes the top is dead. Sometimes it is really quite alive and full. Sometimes new tops are formed as the old ones die away, as in high desert or alpine locations.

The Angle of the Branches

In young trees in a calm area, branches have a tendency to grow upright. Plants growing from the forest floor will grow branches at approximately a forty-five degree angle. This is the typical shape in younger trees and is seen often in nature. See **fig. 1-7**. As the tree ages, the branches have a tendency to flatten out. Branches take on weight of their own and begin to draw down. Snow load, frost, and ice start to bring branches down over time. Create this illusion of age in bonsai by training branches down, as is seen in the tree in **fig. 1-8**. Compare this tree

Fig. 1-8.

to the younger one in the previous photograph and it is clear how the positioning of the branches, particularly the angle of the branches as they come from the trunk, contributes to the illusion of age. The young tree looks young because of the upright angle of the branches. The older tree looks old because the branches are coming out in a more or less horizontal fashion. Continue to age the bonsai by bringing the branches down even further, well below horizontal, to start getting an alpine effect.

Style Combinations

Fig. 1-9 shows a tree that exhibits several different styles at the same time. A highly angular trunk leans out in an extreme slanting style, yet the tree terminates in a very upright form that is reminiscent of the formal upright. The lower branches are slightly weeping, as might be seen on a weeping-style tree. The branches are swept down, not because it's a weeping variety, but because the tree is growing under such adverse conditions that the snow load

Fig. 1-7. An example of a dead apex.

8

Fig. 1-9.

Fig. 1-10.

has forced the lower branches to hug the surface of the ground. If this tree were planted in a fairly tall pot, the lower branches would actually extend over the side of the pot and it could be easily styled into a semi-cascade style. One tree can have several different characteristics and exhibit many different styles simultaneously. It is quite possible to combine styles in many different ways.

Fig. 1-10 shows a classic formal upright tree in a windy area. While the trunk itself is strictly vertical, the prevailing wind, which blows from left to right, has caused not only some dead wood to appear on the top of the tree, but some dead sections of branches toward the wind as well. The branches that are growing away from the wind are encouraged and it gives the tree a certain amount of asymmetry. This is still a formal upright tree, but it is easy to combine the formal upright style with the windswept style.

Bonsai presents many style combinations. A maple tree normally grows with its branches upright. As the tree ages, the branches will be brought

down a bit and new tops may succeed where others have failed. An upright style can be more or less informal. It is difficult to categorize trees that are a combination of styles. Sometimes beautiful trees combine several styles so well it is impossible to pigeonhole them into a single style. The important thing to remember about the formal upright style is that it is one of five inclinations of the trunk. As a style in itself, it can be combined with other styles, such as the octopus style, exposed root style, or root over rock, which is discussed later. Landscapes sometimes have formal upright trees. The important thing is that the trunk is vertical.

THREE IMPORTANT DESIGN ELEMENTS

The Root Buttress

In nature, a tree seed might be deposited in bird droppings or dispersed by the wind. Some seeds can stick in the coats of furry creatures and be deposited at remote distances, but in all these plants, the seed is not buried very deeply. In the nursery trade, the tendency is to transplant seedlings from pot to pot, always planting them just a little bit deeper than is healthful. In healthy bonsai, the root buttress is exposed just as in nature.

Imagine yourself walking through the woods stumbling over exposed roots on the trail. The trees you see all around you have their roots visible to the eye. These roots spread out on all sides of the trunk, giving support to it. This not only functions well to make sure that the tree stays upright, but it's quite aesthetically pleasing to have the widest part of the trunk exposed right at the soil surface. Bonsai that do not have this widening at the bottom of the trunk look unstable. They look as if a branch had been plunged down into the soil in the container. They don't look alive. Contrast this with a bonsai that displays a flared-out trunk at its base. The viewer immediately gets a sense of age and grandeur about the tree. The tree looks balanced, it looks stable, and it looks old.

For this reason try to display as much root buttress on trees as possible. The root buttress represents one of three important design considerations for finding the front of the tree. Displaying a bonsai with roots pointing toward the viewer gives a distracting feeling. Roots splayed out to the right and left side give a sense of calm and stability; the tree presents itself well to the viewer, without having a root poking straight out.

The Trunk Line

The trunk line is important to design. In a formal upright tree, it is quite easy to establish a pleasing trunk line. For other styles where the trunk bends to and fro, there are nice ways to present these curves to the viewer as well as less pleasing aspects. Fortunately for the formal upright tree, which is straight up and down, the trunk line is going to look equally nice from all sides. In the formal upright, the trunk line happens to be smooth and symmetrical so it is not difficult to locate the front of the tree. Often it looks nice from many directions. This is not the case with curved trunks; therefore, it is harder to find the front of the tree. Trunks that curve toward the viewer and then back are very unpleasant. It always looks as though the tree is falling backwards. Trunks that sway evenly from side to side are uninteresting. Trees that curve straight toward the viewer can not be seen easily. The viewer has to duck his head down to look up underneath the tree to observe the trunk line. These trees will always look as though they are falling forward.

The Apex

Most often in nature it is easy to identify the top of a tree. But it is not so obvious when designing bonsai from nursery stock. Sometimes it is difficult to identify the best apex of a tree among the many branches available. When you are designing your tree, keep in mind that the tree must have one specific apex. If it has several potential tops, a suitable one must be chosen and enhanced so that it dominates. A tree with several tops is confusing. It is difficult for the eye to trace the trunk line.

The apex of the tree in **fig. 1-13** is clear and distinct. It is a bright gray

Fig. 1-11. An oak tree buttress, quercus robur, *showing the correct side-to-side root position in the front.*

Fig. 1-12.

visible in your bonsai: a nicely displayed root buttress, a defined trunk line, and a specific apex.

THE FORMAL UPRIGHT AS A DESIGN MODEL

The formal upright style is the first bonsai design to consider. This chapter goes into great detail because most of the bonsai design principles here are applicable to all the other bonsai styles.

dead top, and it is quite visible to the viewer. If you were to start out with a bushy landscape tree that you had acquired from a nursery, the top wouldn't be as obvious as this from the start. In designing bonsai make sure the apex is clearly defined. Look over your finished design and make sure that these three design elements are

Fig. 1-14. Formal upright Japanese larch, **larix kaempferi.** *Note the strong root buttress.*

Fig. 1-13.

Important Proportions

When you see trees in nature, you take it for granted that a tree has certain inherent proportions. In dealing with nursery stock, sometimes these proportions are easy to forget. Generally, the lowest branches are the oldest and, progressing upward, the branches are younger. This establishes a certain size relationship to the trunk and a size relationship from branch to branch. Keep some of these natural proportions in mind while designing bonsai.

The Number One Branch

Teachers of bonsai often stylize or exaggerate the formal upright style in order to give students a sense of proportion. Bonsai is the art of learning how to convert a shrubby nursery tree into an older, more natural style. These exaggerated rules are necessary in order to teach beginners how to style their trees. I firmly believe that once the rules are learned, they are made to be broken. The following rules about the branches on a tree, their proportion and their placement, are designed to help the reader learn a sense of proportion; to overcome his or her fear of pruning a tree. Once the bonsai hobbyist feels comfortable designing trees, the rules that no longer suit his purposes can be discarded. With that in mind, let's look at the importance of the number one branch in bonsai design.

The number one branch is always the lowest branch on the tree. In the formal upright style, it is usually a horizontal branch above the soil surface, often found about a third of the way up toward the top of the tree. It is best displayed coming out from the trunk, proceeding toward the right- or left-hand side of the tree. It is too hidden when placed in back; and when it proceeds straight toward the viewer, the trunk is not visible.

Fig. 1-15 shows an older conifer with its array of branches coming out from the sides of the trunk. The branches are heavier toward the bottom of the tree because they are older. The spaces between these branches are larger. Proceeding toward the top of the tree, the space between branches becomes smaller and smaller until the top of the tree, where it is difficult to see the trunk at all because of new sprouts coming out near the apex. The number one branch should be the lowest, thickest, oldest, longest branch and should contain the most foliage mass. All other branches will be copies of this one in angle and design, except that they will

Fig. 1-15.

all be progressively smaller proceeding up the trunk toward the top of the tree.

Establishing the size of the number one branch helps design the rest of the tree. If the number one branch proceeds from the trunk in a horizontal fashion, the other branches should proceed from the trunk in a horizontal fashion as well. When working with material such as deciduous trees, a slightly uprighted number one branch is appropriate because of the lack of snow load in winter. If the number one branch proceeds out from the trunk at an angle of 30 degrees above horizontal, it makes sense to duplicate this angle in all the other branches on the tree.

Trees that have this consistency of angle also have a more consistent design communicated to the viewer. If the number one branch proceeds out from the trunk well below horizontal, this establishes an alpine or weeping effect and the other branches should follow suit. A number one branch that is bent down heavily looks best when it's complemented by other branches that continue that theme. It is inconsistent to change this angle, except perhaps at the very uppermost part of the tree where the fresh young branches are young.

The Number Two Branch

Once you have established the front of your tree by identifying the apex, the trunk line, and the root buttress, the number one branch establishes an angle, which is important to the number two branch. The number two branch should proceed from the trunk at a higher level than the number one branch. When the number two branch is directly opposite the trunk from the number one branch, it forms an unpleasant bar branch, or an effect like a cross. In design terms, this is quite unsettling. In nature, this rarely happens. One branch will be favored over another. We often see a strong branch on the right side of the tree and a very weak branch on the other. As the tree ages, the number one branch will dominate the design of the tree by sheer size alone. The number two branch, likewise, will shade the other side of the trunk, making it impossible for branches to thrive below it. Alternating back and forth along the tree, each branch will reach out for its own area of sunlight, creating a pinwheel fashion proceeding from the base of the trunk

Fig. 1-16.

to the top of the tree. The number two branch is important because it reinforces the design scheme that you have established with the number one branch.

Fig. 1-16 shows a tree that has a more or less horizontal pattern of branches. Spaces between the branches decrease going up the trunk. The apex is fairly well defined because it becomes harder to see the trunk itself. This spacing is important in bonsai design. Spaces between lower branches should be wide and large. Proceeding toward the top of the tree, the spaces decrease until, finally, the branches all cluster together at the apex. The number two branch should proceed from the trunk at a slightly higher level on the opposite side from the number one branch. This presents to the viewer a very nice trunk in an asymmetrical fashion that is pleasing to the eye.

The Back Branch

The third-lowest branch on the tree should give the tree some depth. Strictly alternating branches from right to left and back to the right would appear redundant and boring. A back branch just slightly higher than the number two branch gives a pleasing depth to a bonsai. Space these back branches so they do not duplicate foliage from the primary branches toward the right side and left side of the tree. Back branches are important because they fill in the empty spaces toward the rear of a tree. It's reasonable to be able to look in and see a tree trunk, but not all the way through a tree. Forward-facing branches are usually found in only the top half of the tree in bonsai design. It is natural to walk around a tree in nature to find the most pleasing angle and enjoy it from that position. So, too, with bonsai. Look at all sides of the tree and try to see the trunk in the bottom half of the tree. If it's not possible to see the trunk in the bottom half of the tree because branches are in the way, the tendency is to move to the right or left in order to be able to get the view. Back branches should not obstruct the view of the trunk.

Ratios

There are other important proportions to consider while designing a tree. Proceed from the largest branch at the base of the tree up to the smallest branch at the top. Remember, the largest branch at the bottom is also the longest branch and the thickest and the oldest. But in pruning nursery material for bonsai, compare the ratio of the size of the trunk to the size of the branch. If they are similar in size, the tree will look young. Visualize trees in nature. See **fig. 1-17**. The size of the trunk is always considerably larger than the diameter of even the largest branch on the tree. Trimming nursery stock so the largest branches are removed early in the life of the tree results in an older-looking bonsai.

Consider a 100-year-old pine tree. If the lowest branch is 99 years old, it would look out of proportion. In the 100 years that the tree was growing the lowest branch died off, to be replaced by younger sprouts. A 100-year-old tree, sporting a 50-year-old number one branch, is more aesthetically pleasing, and we should copy this with our bonsai. This principle can obviously be carried to extremes. A very old tree with extremely young branches is not pleasing to look at, either. A good balance between the size of the trunk and the lowest branch can be achieved by keeping the diameter of the lowest branch about half the diameter of the trunk. This gives a pleasing effect, like what is seen in nature. Notice the branches in the illustration. They are considerably smaller than the trunk. This gives a feeling of age and grandeur. It makes the trunk look important and makes the branches look as though they have been on the trunk for the right length of time.

THE FOLIAGE TRIANGLE

Definitions and Parameters

The Bottom Third
One can imagine an imaginary triangle formed by these three points: the apex, the tip of the number one branch, and the tip of the number two branch. Try to establish all your foliage within this triangle. This imaginary triangle may be irregularly shaped, but it always contains these three points. Consider for a moment the foliage within this imaginary triangle. The trunk should be visible in its entirety in the bottom third. So should the major branches of the tree. Adjacent to the trunk, these branches should be slightly bare. The angle of these branches should be visible and their consistency in angle and style obvious. It should be easy to observe that the bottom branch is the largest and that other branches are progressively smaller in diameter.

The Middle Third
In the middle third of this imaginary foliage triangle, the trunk should be visible about half the time, slightly ob-

Fig. 1-17.

structed by branches radiating out toward the viewer, interrupting the trunk line somewhat. An imaginary viewing point is found halfway from the top of the tree to the root buttress. This point on the tree is where the eye level should be as you admire your bonsai. Obviously, if you have a taller bonsai, a shorter table is necessary in order to keep this imaginary viewpoint at eye level. A table that is 40 inches (100 cm) high will raise most bonsai to the correct eye level.

The Top Third

The top third of the foliage triangle is usually thick with foliage. The trunk is not visible at all. The top third of the foliage triangle usually forms the base of the apex of the tree. It is a dense collection of branches that are young, thick, and vibrant. The apex of the tree does not have to be sharp and pointed. Often the apex of a tree consists of dense clouds of foliage which combine to form the top third of the foliage triangle.

THE BRANCH

Secondary and Tertiary Ramifications

Ancient branches sometimes display a great deal of twigginess, as in **fig. 1-18**. Even though most of the branch is dead, this is an important design detail in bonsai. Branches that just proceed outward in a long, straight fashion, with little change in shape, size, or direction, form an uninteresting design. In pruning, try to develop these secondary ramifications. In deciduous trees, it is extremely important to develop a large number of secondary and tertiary branches so the tree in winter looks just as beautiful as it does with the leaves present.

The View from Above

Looking down from the top of a bonsai branch should show the shape of an-

other small bonsai. The beginning of the branch should look like the trunk of a small tree, and the secondary, tertiary, and smaller branchlets should create what look like branches on an imaginary bonsai, viewed from up above. This degree of detail contributes to the beauty and the illusion of age of a bonsai.

The View from the Side

Branches viewed from the side form a fairly flat bottom, ideally showing the woody part of the branch on the underside but not on the top. Leaves should proceed from the branch upward as they face the light. Branches look nicer if downward-directed branches and foliage are pruned and pinched away. Vertically directed branches above the foliage cloud should be pruned away for a more or less horizontal pattern. The tip of the branch should be slightly raised, even if the branch is trained below horizontal. This gives the tree a fine look and conveys a feeling of strength and health.

Fig. 1-18.

Differing Angles as You Approach the Top of the Tree

As branches become younger toward the top of the tree, they become more uplifted on their ends. Strong, horizontal branches at the base of the tree are appropriate. The side of a branch on the lower part of a tree should have a silhouette that is quite isolated. Approaching the top of the tree, foliage on the branch will be closer to the trunk as the branch gets shorter and younger.

JIN, SHARI, AND SABA MIKI

Definitions

It is important to be able to describe the location, type, and size of deadwood on our trees. Of the many definitions for deadwood, *jin* seems to be the one most often used. When deadwood appears at the top of a tree, there is no question that most people in bonsai will call it *jin*. Deadwood on the side of a branch is *shari*. *Saba miki* indicates deadwood on the trunk of a tree. Certain trees normally display these design features. A hollowed-out apple tree or oak tree is common in nature, and this is known as *saba miki* in order to help describe its location and extent.

The *jin* in **fig. 1-19** is quite obvious. The bright, dead top is pleasing to the eye and worth copying on a bonsai. **Fig. 1-20** shows trees that have not only *jin* but *shari* as well. Notice the pleasing effect of having dead branches along a tree and note its contribution to the illusion of age. **Fig. 1-21** shows yet a more severe example of *jin*. Not only is the top of the tree dead, but lots of *shari* grace the sides and the tree abounds with *saba miki*. In fact, the whole tree is deadwood but still beautiful to behold. Try to copy these effects on bonsai by carving areas so they look like these natural driftwood shapes. Notice the amount of detail. The tree in **fig. 1-22** is quite dramatic,

Fig. 1-19.

Fig. 1-20.

even though it's completely dead. Its shape is really beautiful. It overlooks a lake. It gives a mental history of the area and its environment. Sometimes deadwood can convey a stronger design than live wood.

Fig. 1-21.

Fig. 1-22.

Different Designs

Jin, *shari*, and *saba miki* appear in all types, sizes, and shapes of trees. The desert has characteristic shapes associated with dryness and heat. The *jin* in the mountains is shaped differently because of the different environmental conditions. Deadwood or driftwood on the coast tends to be curved and wind-swept, very different from deadwood in a calm area. Similarly, the *jin*, *shari*, and *saba miki* at a lakeside differ from those at the edge of a stream. Learn from nature how to carve bonsai so the deadwood is consistent with the live wood. This gives us consistency of style, and gives us a more pleasing style.

RECOMMENDED SPECIES

Outline Shapes

Fig. 1-23 shows a nursery plant with a typical pine shape, slightly taller than it is wide. This is a modestly strong upright grower. The trunk that is visible on this specimen is straight and upright, a fine candidate for the formal

upright style. Pay attention to outline shapes of nursery trees. Strong upright growers are quite obvious because they are so much taller than they are wide. Look inside the branches and examine the trunk line of a tree that is much wider than it is tall to see whether it is straight. Often it will not be. Plants

Fig. 1-23.

that are wider than they are tall usually have curved trunks and are not candidates for the formal upright style.

Hormones and Growth

The outline shape is an indication where growth hormone is concentrated in the plant. A tree that is much taller than it is wide has a concentration of growth hormone in the leading tip. Such an outline indicates a fine candidate for one of the strong upright styles and an unlikely candidate for a cascading type of tree.

Some common plants for the formal upright-style bonsai include fir, spruce, hemlock, and most palm trees. Also included in this group of plants are cedars and arborvitae. Cryptomeria from Japan is a strong upright grower and usually has a trunk that grows quite straight and tall. The larch has an outline shape similar to that of maple because both are deciduous. But larch is also a conifer and a somewhat strong upright grower and could be used for the formal upright style. Often the only difference in shape between a pine and a larch is that larch branches are more upright. A pine will have horizontal branches. Both make fine formal upright trees. Other strong upright growers are sequoias and redwoods.

OUTLINE SHAPES

The Flame Shape

This shape is often seen in arborvitae and Italian cypress and resembles the flame of a candle. The poplar tree makes a wonderful flame shape naturally and, in bonsai, is unique. The natural shape of the conifers in **fig. 1-24** suggests that the flame shape is useful in designing any strong upright-growing conifer.

Fig. 1-24.

The Inverted Heart Shape

Many stone-fruit trees, such as peach, plum, and cherry, have this outline shape. Within the scope of the formal upright design, secondary twigging and branches help to create this shape. This is the design in crab apple, as well as oak. The inverted heart shape comes from having a slightly pointed crown with low secondary branches that grow below the lowest branches as they reach for light, creating the heart shape.

The Ball Shape

Boxwood is a good example of the ball shape as it grows naturally. Lots of pines will grow just as high as they do wide, thereby creating the outline shape resembling a globe or a ball. Many elms also grow just as tall as they do wide. **Fig. 1-25** shows an elm that has been grown as an upright style with horizontal branches, but the tree is basically as high as it is wide, and starts to resemble a ball shape.

Fig. 1-25.

The Triangle Shape

All high-altitude species, particularly the alpine fir, Englemann spruce, and other taller conifers that grow in adverse conditions, have this heavy triangular shape. It is characterized by a very pointed top and branches brought down close to the trunk due to snow load.

The Inverted Triangle Shape

The broom style associated with elm and with the zelkova gives an inverted triangle shape because branches are rising from a single trunk and coming up to a rounded apex. The trunk divides into two branches and those branches divide into four. Those four divide into eight and so forth, creating the broom effect so that the top of the triangle is at the apex of the tree. The tree is at its widest point there. This forms the inverted foliage triangle.

The Elongated Shape

Any plant that is wider than it is tall can be used for a formal upright, provided the trunk is straight, such as bonsai azaleas, which naturally want to grow really wide. They still retain an apex that is directly over the trunk and root buttress. Pines are often pruned into this shape in order to display long lower branches over a pond in the Japanese garden.

The Prostrate Shape

Any weeping variety of plant, for example the procumbens juniper, will make an excellent prostrate bonsai. To make them into a formal upright, stake them up to train them in order to establish a straight trunk. The branches will naturally form the weeping or prostrate shape.

TRAINING THE TREE

Pruning with the Pinch-and-Grow Technique

There are basically two ways to train bonsai. One is to direct growth by pinching back new growth as it appears. When the secondary growth appears, keep the new shoots that are going in the desired direction and rub away the others. Continue this process over several years, and it is possible to train an entire tree without ever using mechanical techniques such as training wire. Compact the growth by pinching back repeatedly. Elongate growth by allowing it to grow. Create trunk movement for all styles simply by pinching back portions of the trunk when it is young and by redirecting new tops as the tree grows.

Training with Wire

It is also possible to train a tree using copper wire. Take the wire and wind it around a branch; then move it in any direction until the branch is in the desired new position. Cut off the wire after about a year to avoid scarring the branch. Clamps, turnbuckles, and the like can be used to bend fairly large branches to style the tree. These

Fig. 1-26.

methods are discussed in Chapters 11 and 12 in greater detail. **Fig. 1-26** shows a model of a young tree that is starting to have its branches moved down by snow load. By using wire to move branches down, it's possible to artificially age trees to simulate alpine material without the use of snow.

SELECTING A CONTAINER

Size

In general, for a pleasing look, select a bonsai container whose length is two-thirds the height of the tree. The height of the container should approximate the diameter of the trunk of the tree or be as close to this proportion as possible. With young plant material, it is difficult to find containers that are shallow enough to complement our trees and we have to wait a few years for the trunk diameter to get larger.

Color

Dull earth colors, brown hues, and un-glazed pots complement evergreens and conifers best. Reserve the bright-colored glazes for bonsai plants that have lots of inherent color. When using a brightly colored pot, do not match the color of the leaf to the color of the pot. For example, red leaves on a maple don't look particularly good in a red pot, but in a contrasting blue pot the red leaves look nice and brilliant.

Design

In considering the general shape of a container, keep in mind that an angular pot looks best with a contorted tree. A curved pot complements a gently undulating bonsai. Pots with legs or lots of decoration look best with trees that are highly detailed. Trees with a very simple design, such as a calm, formal upright, look best in a shallow oval container that does not contain lots of design features.

Texture

Some pots are highly textured. This texture complements the texture of bark or the texture of branches on a bonsai. A very smooth pot looks best with a smooth-barked tree. Try to match the ruggedness of the pot with the texture of the tree for best results.

GROOMING FOR A SHOW

The Pot

Remove the tree and clean the container well, using a mild abrasive and some light detergent or bleach. Rinse the container many times to make sure that chemical residues do not remain on the sides of the container. Rub a light application of mineral oil on unglazed containers for a little bit of added sheen. Clean containers make plants look their best.

The Tree

Make sure that the tree is weed-free, that the front is displayed properly, and that no fallen needles or leaves appear on the soil surface. Moss should cover only about half the soil surface. Larger amounts of moss are detrimental to the health of the bonsai. Consider the design of the tree. On a dry landscape with juniper, the presence of moss is perhaps inappropriate. Allow moss to appear only on trees that evoke a landscape that is stable and moist.

The Stand

Choose a stand that will display bonsai at the proper level. Remember the viewing point, the imaginary point halfway between the base of the trunk and the top of the tree. Try to come as close as possible to achieving the proper height. Don't force viewers to duck to look underneath the tree. Also, a plant that is too high is distracting to the total display. Choose a stand that complements the color of the tree and the pot. A loud, garish-looking, brightly colored stand can distract the eye from a nice presentation. Its size should be comfortably larger than the pot that it holds. A stand that is too small looks crowded and cramped. A stand that is too large makes a tree look insignificant. Stand textures should complement the pot and the tree. A stand with much inlay and carving will detract from a simple planting of formal upright.

THE INFORMAL UPRIGHT STYLE
Moyogi

THE FIVE BASIC STYLES

The Formal Upright

As seen in the previous chapter, the formal upright has no inclination to the trunk. It is aesthetically the most stable. It evokes calm. It suggests lack of adversity in the environmental conditions surrounding the tree. The formal upright lends itself well to tall trees, as well as to trees that naturally grow strongly upright. These conditions vary in nature. The Douglas fir, for example, normally grows as a strong upright tree in the calm, coastal inlands of the Pacific Northwest. However, this normally upright tree, when subjected to the winds of the Pacific Ocean or the high deserts of eastern Oregon or the adverse conditions found in the higher altitudes of the Cascades, can assume quite distorted growth. It is possible for a normally upright tree to grow quite curved under the conditions of environmental stress.

The Informal Upright

The informal upright is a fine example of a curved bonsai style duplicating curving trunks found in nature. A tree that might normally grow quite straight might swing widely to and fro under certain stressful conditions. **Fig. 2-1** shows a Murrayana pine from the Oregon Cascades that is highly distorted due to its growing conditions. The trunk starts out upright from the base and swings from side to side before the apex finally stabilizes itself above the root buttress. This is classic *moyogi* style. The tree represents recovery from adversity. This style epitomizes the concept of balance.

In **fig. 2-2**, a mountain hemlock grows in a rock crevice. This area has

Fig. 2-1.

Fig. 2-2.

very little rainfall, bright light, and a great deal of snow load. These forces have shaped this tree over time. Normally, the mountain hemlock would grow fairly upright with its branches gently sweeping down because of snow. This tree has been forced to grow to the left, then abruptly to the right, in order to balance itself in this situation. The trunk has become curved, as shown.

In **fig. 2-3** is a tree in a completely different environment. Here a conifer is bending toward the light over the top of a waterfall at a much lower altitude. This is a lowland stream moving toward the Oregon coastline at an eleva-

Fig. 2-3.

tion of about 1,000 feet (300 m). Erosion has created a bit of instability for the root system on the edge of the precipice. The tree has gradually leaned toward the water, not because water is there, but because of erosion in the root system itself. The more the tree leaned toward the water, the more it wanted to right itself. What has been created is classic *moyogi* style, characterized by the overcoming of its adversity. The root system is now firmly entrenched in this rock and the apex is directly above the root system. Models like this from nature help in designing bonsai trees.

The Slanting Style

In the classic slanting style is a tree that has not completely overcome its adversity. This occurs in the presence of erosion, where the tree is slanting out toward water, or slanting out to reach toward light, but the apex is not over the root system. It may never recover.

The Semi-Cascade Style

This style in nature shows not so much an attempt by a whole tree to overcome adversity but the lowest branches trying to recover where the apex could not. This is a different approach to styling bonsai, trying to duplicate something unusual that happens in nature. Sometimes the apex of the tree is subject to drought, perhaps too much wind, perhaps too much ultraviolet light. Year after year, the top tries to grow and thrive, but every year it fails. The lower parts of the tree, on the other hand, are more successful because they are closer to the ground. They are protected from the wind, and they are protected from high amounts of ultraviolet light from the sun. They are also less subject to drought because of the decreased passage of air over their surfaces. If trees try to grow next to a vertical precipice, it is quite possible that the lowest branches will reach downward rather than upward, even though that is what would be normally found in a tree of this type.

The Formal Cascade Style

The formal cascade style is a continuation of the same conditions that created the semi-cascade, only more extreme. Most formal cascades copy trees that are high on mountaintops, clinging to the edges of rocky gorges, or are clinging to a boulder at the side exposed to coastal winds. The lower branches succeed better because they hug the ground, and will, over time, progress down along the soil surface. In order to plant this style of bonsai in a container, use a cascading pot that allows the lowest branches to hang down below the container, just as the lower branches would hang down below the rocky

ledge up in the gorge from where we get our inspiration.

THE *MOYOGI* STYLE

This bonsai style represents the ultimate in stability in the face of adversity. It is indicative of the plant's ability to recover from the environmental conditions in which it grows. This style of bonsai is the most popular one today. The majority of both Japanese bonsai and Chinese *p'en t'sai* are *moyogi* style. It is popular in Japan as a symbol of the Noh play. It is often seen in silhouette behind this form of Japanese opera. It is the most-often-seen style both in the United States and the rest of the world.

In **fig. 2-4** the silhouette of a pine tree grows out of the top of a rock, above 4,000 feet (1,200 m) in elevation. This tree has been subjected to the most extreme conditions. The trunk has started off to the right, and then was forced to lean sharply to the left. The tree finally recovered so the top is over where the root base originates. The seed was originally dropped almost directly below where the top of this trunk now exists.

Fig. 2-4.

VARIATIONS ON THE *MOYOGI*

The Eroded Tree

Fig. 2-5 shows some of the results of erosion on a tree's roots. This tree on the coast has been subjected to a great deal of wind, 45 inches (115 cm) of annual rainfall, multiple storms, and

Fig. 2-5.

Fig. 2-6.

shifting sands. The tree's roots continue to survive because of the moisture provided by the sandy soil and high annual rainfall. The trunk tries to recover, points itself toward the light, and protects its branches against the onslaught of the prevailing wind. The tree survives in spite of this adversity, creating this spectacular driftwood effect on its roots. This is a type of *moyogi* because the adversity caused by erosion has been overcome. Other *moyogi* styles can be caused by other conditions.

The Windswept Tree

Fig. 2-6 shows a classic *moyogi* that has been formed by wind alone. This lakeside tree has plenty of moisture during the summer and plenty of snowfall during the winter to protect it, but in spite of these conditions, it is continually forced to try to regain its balance because of the prevailing wind that comes from left to right. Often, there is evidence of many trunks that tried to succeed against the wind and failed. Branches that tried to point toward the

wind and are now dry and shriveled may be seen. This magnificent example of *moyogi* shows how nature's forces can shape a tree, and yet the tree becomes more beautiful because it survives the challenge. This tree recovers from these stresses and therefore is classified as a *moyogi*, rather than a slanting style. If the wind had pushed this tree continually over from left to right, a slanting style would be formed. This apex has recovered quite nicely year after year. It tries to right itself and creates a magnificent design.

The Alpine Tree

The tree in **fig. 2-7** is a beautiful, very old example of what happens at high altitudes. This tree is surviving in the Oregon Cascades at over one mile in elevation. For only a brief period of time, this tree is able to get light from underneath the snow, under which it is buried for ten months of the year. When the tree is finally able to reach out to the sun, it grows quickly and then goes dormant. This tree is, perhaps, thousands of years old, and it is a classic *moyogi* style, because the trunk undulates from right to left and from

Fig. 2-7.

left to right, but always tries to re-cover. The apex still remains over the root buttress and it is a beautiful, well balanced tree. The many tops that it has produced are what make the alpine *moyogi* distinct from the windswept *moyogi* and the eroded-tree *moyogi*, previously described.

In the alpine tree *moyogi*, the trunk curves because of the large number of unsuccessful apices it produces. The snow load that brings down the branches is also responsible for pro-tecting this tree. A new top will emerge from the snow and start to grow rap-idly because of the moisture available to the roots. The tree grows rapidly but, because of excess ultraviolet light at 5,000 feet (1500 m) in altitude and because of excess wind under these conditions, the top dries up and fails. Down below, some of the branches are yet protected by snow. They remain green and are eager to create a new top in the absence of the failed apex above.

TRAINING AND BENDING METHODS

For Branches

Fig. 2-8 shows the natural shape of stressed branches under extreme envi-ronmental conditions. To design a bon-sai that copies nature, it is necessary to bend branches down in an extreme style, as shown in the illustration. With training skills and carving skills, it's possible to take both live and dead branches and copy these shapes in or-der to evoke, to the viewer, the experi-ence of happening across such a tree in the mountains.

Deadwood can be moved if it is heated slowly in the presence of water. One method is to wrap the branch in wet towels and heat it slowly with a soldering iron or steam. These are the same methods used by furniture-makers to produce bentwood for such things as rocking chairs. It is possible to take dead branches from a bonsai and move them, even though they are brittle, simply by softening them with steam. By heating the water impreg-

Fig. 2-8.

nated in the branch, it will move without breaking.

Much easier to accomplish is getting live branches to move while they are still supple, moving them down into positions evocative of **fig. 2-8**. Then the branches are intentionally killed by stripping off the bark. Once the bark has been stripped off, wire can be placed around the dead branch while it is still supple. The branch is moved into the appropriate position and allowed to die out over time. In the summer months, this process only takes a few weeks to complete. Once the branch is fused into position by desiccation, the wire can be cut off and the branch treated with lime sulfur to create a driftwood effect, as well as to preserve the wood from rotting.

Fig. 2-10. This bonsai clamp is adding a bend to this trunk line to correct a straight section in the **moyogi**.

Trunks

The magnificent *saba miki* shown in **fig. 2-9** can be duplicated on bonsai by carving. Some techniques that I like to use are to hollow out the side of a trunk with a rotary tool and to smooth out the edges with various carving knives and chisels. The live cambium layer around this injury tries to protect itself and creates a very nice hollow effect. A very uninteresting nursery plant can be made to look like an old hollowed-out oak tree by being carved in this manner. I like to keep pieces of driftwood in my workshop as examples of nature's carving. I can copy its form and its style on a live bonsai tree as I stare at the example of driftwood only

Fig. 2-11.

Fig. 2-9.

a few inches away. This helps me visualize the texture and the curves that are necessary to make the carving more realistic.

As an exercise, I would recommend to bonsai carvers to try to make a common piece of wood, such as a section of 2 × 4, look just like a fine driftwood carving that you might pick up at the beach. If you can take a foot-long (30 cm) 2 × 4 and carve it so it looks like an intricately carved piece of driftwood from the tree in the illustration, you will indeed succeed as a bonsai driftwood carver.

Branchlets

The many branchlets shown in **fig. 2-12** are fine examples of the secondary and tertiary ramifications so prized in bonsai. This illustration is a live Sitka spruce on the U.S. West Coast. This highly windswept tree is alive and doing well. What this illustration shows is the number of times this branch has tried to put out new buds and has failed. The effect is quite startling and remarkable. Duplicating deadwood as detailed as this will result in a truly remarkable bonsai. This amount of detail contributes to the illusion of age. Deadwood doesn't always have to be smooth and polished.

Deadwood should alternate between the very refined and the extremely detailed. If at all possible, in carving a live branch into a dead *jin* or *saba miki*, try to preserve the twigginess of the branch. These details can make a tremendous amount of difference in the success of the design.

Roots

In illustration **2-13** is a lakeside tree that has survived centuries of high altitude and all the adverse conditions that accompany that location. Notwithstanding late snow, early frost, a high amount of rainfall, and severe erosion, this tree has survived because its roots have dug in, in spite of having been eroded away heavily. Multiple branches and roots are exposed above the soil surface, and yet the tree survives, and it is a magnificent example of the *moyogi* style, which represents success against environmental adversity.

Fig. 2-13.

Fig. 2-12.

27

THE FOLIAGE TRIANGLE

The previous chapter described the three points making up this imaginary triangle: the tip of the apex, the tip of the number one branch, and the tip of the number two branch. **Fig. 2-14** presents a classic *moyogi* style growing in lava at high altitude. It exhibits a well-defined foliage triangle. Easily visible are the number one branch, the number two branch, and the apex. All the foliage is concentrated within the triangle formed by these three points. In designing bonsai, we use examples like this from nature to create very pleasing forms.

Fig. 2-14.

Branch Position

As the illustration shows, the branches that proceed from the outside of the curve of the trunk tend to dominate those branches that instead proceed from the inside of the curve. This makes sense. Imagine looking down onto the top of a tree. It is much easier to see branches that proceed from the outside of a curve than if they proceed from the inside. Exposed branches thus have an advantage. They are warmer. They receive more ultraviolet light and therefore are able to process more nutrients and sunlight for the tree.

As discussed above, if two branches proceed from the trunk at the same point, one branch usually dominates. A branch that proceeds from the outside of a curve naturally is going to dominate any branch that proceeds from the inside. Over time this forms the classic *moyogi* style, which is to have a branch at these junctures. It is possible to do this artificially with nursery stock. Place a stiff wire around the trunk of a young sapling and bend it every which way to create a classic *moyogi* curve to the trunk. Then select the branches that will succeed with the curving. Outside each curve, put a branch or a branch bud. Encourage these branches.

Deciduous versus Evergreen

With deciduous trees, obviously there is no snow load. The winter arrives, the foliage drops off, and there is very little for snow to attach itself to. On deciduous trees, many branches proceed upward at about a 30-degree angle above horizontal. These classic angles are the natural style of maples, elms, and fruit trees.

The evergreen retains its foliage, in spite of snow, ice, and winter storms. The weight of ice and snow on a branch is a major stressor. In time, the branches are drawn strongly downward in high desert or alpine regions. Examine the tree in **fig. 2-15** again. Notice the angle of the branches as they proceed from the trunk. This evergreen, because of the extreme snow load each winter, has its branches bent considerably downward. Where a maple or elm might have its branches proceed out from the trunk 30 degrees above horizontal, this tree has its branches proceed from the trunk at approximately 30 degrees below horizontal. This is typical of evergreen trees in stressful situations.

The pine in **fig. 2-16** has its lower branches brought down because of snow load, but the apex of the tree is still quite young and is free from the weight of the snow in winter because of the overall height of the tree. The apex for most of the winter months is visible above the snow pack. This tree is growing at approximately 3,000 feet

Fig. 2-15.

Fig. 2-16.

(900 m) in altitude and the average snow pack in this area is normally less than five feet high. This tree is about nine feet (2.7 m) high; therefore, the top four feet (1.2 m) still exhibit the youth of a younger tree, in spite of the fact that this tree is probably centuries old. The tree exhibits the classic

moyogi leans and undulations, the apex is still over the root ball, and it is a magnificent example of recovery from adversity.

Exaggeration of Angle

The previous example from nature exhibits extreme bends in the tree due to extreme environmental conditions. **Fig. 2-17** shows a bonsai grown from nursery stock that is not subject to these extreme curves. When this tree was first wired several years ago, it was wired into a classic *moyogi* style and the branches were shaped to proceed from the outside of the curves. This is a Scotch pine, which is a strong, upright grower. Once the training wire was removed from the trunk, the tree started to straighten itself out. I have not been able to restore the original curves that I put in this trunk, because now the trunk is too large.

In training *moyogi* style, it is important to exaggerate the curves in a tree. Trees naturally will try to recover from these bends over time, and it is a shame to lose the original bends that you designed for your tree. I highly recommend bending the tree a bit more than what you feel comfortable doing. Once

Fig. 2-17.

the clamps are off, once the turn-buckles are removed or the wire cut off, the tree will try to revert to its natural state. It is very difficult, after a few years, to try to restore the same amount of curve that you had originally intended for the tree. In the illustration above, I wish I had exaggerated those curves more, because instead of a classic *moyogi* style, I have a tree with a mild slanting style. I appreciate the style for what it is, but it is a bit disturbing to remember what the tree used to look like only five years ago.

It is important to note that certain species of tree have a tendency to restore their shape more than others. I have had to bend some trees more severely than others because of their natural tendency to revert to their original form. Some trees that are very difficult to train are the bristlecone pine, the pinyon pine, the alpine fir, the Alberta spruce, and the shimpaku juniper. Limber pine, murrayana pine, lodgepole pine, and gingko are similarly resistant to training. I recommend exaggerating their curves while styling with wire and making sure that the wire remains on the tree for at least two years before removal. Otherwise, the tree will tend to restore itself to its natural shape in only a few months after training.

TRUNK MOVEMENT

Fig. 2-18 shows a classic example of the undulating movement found in fine *moyogi*-style bonsai. It is a shimpaku juniper many years old. The branches proceed from the outsides of the curves, and a gradual taper from the root buttress to the apex is quite pleasing to the eye.

Fig. 2-19 shows a Japanese maple that has classic *moyogi* style, leaning to the right and then coming back to the left. The apex is over the root buttress and this symbolizes recovery from adversity. The next illustration, **fig. 2-20**, shows just the reverse curve, where the trunk proceeds in the opposite direction and yet still recovers. This latter maple is a vine maple, several hundred years old.

Fig. 2-18.

Fig. 2-19.

30

Fig. 2-20.

THE SLANTING STYLE

Shakan

DESIGN CONSIDERATIONS

Sho-Shakan

Fig. 3-1 shows a wonderful example of a *sho-shakan* tree. The *sho-shakan* is a trunk which is only slightly slanting. Unlike the *moyogi*, the trunk does not completely recover. It slants off to one side and the apex is not over the bulk of the rootage of the plant. In the slightly slanting style, or *sho-shakan* style, a slight inclination leads to the possibility of visual instability. Notice, however, in the illustration, the volume of rootage which gives it strength in the rock. In the long, low number one branch, which tends to give visual balance to the tree, notice in particular the

Fig. 3-1.

strong foliage triangle. In talking about bonsai design, it is easy to forget that the designs come directly from nature. This fine specimen is an excellent example of how to learn from nature to design a very nice *sho-shakan*.

In **fig. 3-2** is an example of *sho-shakan* in a multiple-trunk planting. These three trunks come up from a single plant. One trunk is completely dead and exhibits an apex *jin*. The base of the root buttress exhibits a fine example of *saba miki* and the slightly windswept effect is pleasing with the inclination of right to left in this slanted style.

Fig. 3-3.

Fig. 3-2.

Chu-Shakan

The tree in **fig. 3-3** is one of the finest examples of a natural *chu-shakan* I have ever seen. This plant must be many centuries old, perhaps more than a thousand years old. Its twisted trunk and branches are a joy to observe and study. The slight inclination of this trunk is more than the *sho-shakan* and should be qualified as a *chu-shakan* or a medium-slanted tree. The slant is caused by the prevailing wind, as well as the direction of the light. The tree is pointing its foliage toward the north. The extreme rocky conditions in which it is growing make it difficult for this tree even to get above the rocky ledge in which it is growing. It is growing in conditions above 6,000 feet (1,800 m) in elevation and is a wonderful example of survival in extreme altitude conditions.

Dai-Shakan

Fig. 3-4 is a good example of the most extreme style of slanting tree, called a *dai-shakan*. The trunk is almost horizontal at some point among its various undulations. The trunk proceeds from extreme right to extreme left, barely above horizontal, and it just clears the ground as it tries to find protection from wind in this extremely exposed location. It is difficult to plant this type of bonsai in a container because of the tendency of the plant to tip over the pot. Choose the container carefully and make sure the pot has enough actual weight as well as visual weight in order to balance this type of planting.

Look at **fig. 3-4** and try to imagine the size and shape container to make this planting a success. This type of planting might best be suited to a miniature landscape, or *saikei*, because the roots could be supported by rocks and the type of container that it would be planted in would be a large oval tray that would include the area below the apex as well as contain the root mass.

Another style in the *dai-shakan* is the literati, or *bunjin*, style. This is an extreme slanting style and yet the plant is trimmed so severely that the weight

Fig. 3-4.

of the branches does not cause the container to tip over when the plant is placed in it. Notice that in all of these examples thus far, the angle of the branches is consistent from side to side in spite of the angle of the trunk. If the angle of the trunk is 45 degrees above horizontal, the branches are still consistent from right to left, with respect to the ground. This is important for visual stability. In designing bonsai, make sure the right and left sides of the tree are balanced in their design.

Fig. 3-5 has an example of a common juniper, *juniperus communis*, that has been grafted with shimpaku juniper. This is a *chu-shakan* design, but notice that the branches on the right-hand side are 20 degrees below horizontal and the branches on the left-hand side are also 20 degrees below horizontal. This is important with the slanting style, to achieve visual stability. Branches trained unevenly from side to side make the tree look as though it is about to fall over. If the branches are consistent with respect to horizontal, regardless of the angle of

Fig. 3-5.

the trunk, visual stability is attained and the design is much more pleasing to look upon.

SURFACE ROOTAGE

Its Biology

Notice the two-trunk tree, *shakan*-style, in **fig. 3-6**. The wide surface rootage that is visible makes this planting look extremely stable, in spite of the fact that both trunks are leaning a bit off the vertical. The planting could be considered a *sho-shakan* because it is not even a medium slant, but to have two trunks leaning away from each other like this, it might appear quite unstable were it not for the surface rootage, which is highly visible.

In **fig. 3-7**, similarly, is what used to be a formal upright tree that has died. The top *jin* has given up and a new apex has formed toward the water. This new apex has come up and converted this tree into a slanting style because of its angle of growth. Notice particularly below, how the rootage

Fig. 3-6.

Fig. 3-7.

contributes to the feeling of visual stability of this tree. Not only is this mechanical stability, but this tree is very comfortable to look at. One can imagine bonsai design that would use this effect. This design would be very pleasing to look upon and can be easily designed. When I go into the woods, I like to imagine trees in containers, not because I want to possess them and bring them home, but because I use natural trees as an exercise in bonsai design. In some of the photographs that I have brought back from the mountains, I have actually drawn in bonsai pots around the trees to help me visualize and to understand proportion and visual stability in bonsai design.

With this particular tree, it is easy to visualize a cup-shaped bonsai container that would house this unusual combination of failed formal upright and successful *sho-shakan*. The biology of surface rootage is simple. In an area where extreme wind or environmental conditions rock the tree, the roots will gradually become stronger. If you rock a branch or a trunk, it becomes thicker.

This same principle applies to roots. In the slanting style, the surface root-age that receives the most light grows the strongest. Those roots that receive light are also the roots that are the most heated by the sun. This heat translates into root growth. The root growth in turn increases the diameter of the roots, and as the diameter of the roots increases, so does the strength of the roots. As the strength of the roots increases, these roots are more and more able to support the weight of an increasingly slanting tree. Eventually, the tree ceases to slant. The apex still remains well outside of the root buttress, but visual stability has been achieved as well as biological stability.

The reverse is also true. Poor rootage underneath a number one branch occurs because the number one branch cools the ground below the branch and root growth is difficult. Vigorous root growth usually will occur elsewhere around the root buttress, but it is usually weakest underneath the number one branch. Keep these design considerations in mind. In developing a slanting style, make sure the predominant rootage is not underneath the number one branch or it will be inconsistent with the principles in nature.

ENVIRONMENTAL DESIGN

Slanting styles are caused by environmental stress. This could be erosion, wind, or snow load. In terms of trunk inclination, the apex is not going to be found over the root buttress. Several things can cause this, but the tree has not been able to recover. If it had been able to recover, it would be *moyogi* style instead of *shakan*. Being a *shakan* has its own special design considerations.

Looking at *shakan* that are in the desert reveals trees that have shifting sands and extreme winds. The branches are still growing horizontal to the ground, but the trunk is inclined toward one side. The branches on the side away from the wind grow stronger than branches that grow toward the wind. Deadwood is found not only at the top of the tree as *jin*, but much *saba miki* and *shari* that face the wind.

The oft seen slanting style at the beach frequently is a slanting tree due to erosion. What is interesting is that quite often a windswept tree at the beach is actually leaning toward the wind and the branches are leaning away from the wind. This is because often wind, rain, and waves tend to erode sand from the rootage of the tree. As this happens, the tree has a tendency to incline itself toward the ocean. Prevailing winds come from the ocean side.

So here is a situation where the tree is inclining itself toward the ocean, inclining itself into the wind. The tree adjusts and is able to pull its branches away from the wind by favoring those buds that are toward the leeward side of the prevailing wind. Here is a *shakan* style that is leaning in one direction and yet has its strongest branches in the other direction. A *shakan* in a windy gorge presents quite the opposite scenario. The prevailing wind usually is not only responsible for sweeping the branches off to one side, but the same conditions are responsible for pushing the apex off to the same side as well.

Fig. 3-8. A good example of a slanted-style weeping bonsai. The tree is golden threadbranch cypress, **chamaecyparis pisifera filifera 'aurea'.**

HOW TO USE ROCKS

Chapter 9 will examine some issues concerning rock plantings, the root over rock style, and some discussion of *saikei*. In this chapter, however, I will mention the role of rocks in stabilizing the slanting trunks in *shakan* style.

In planting bonsai from nursery stock the decision to use the slanting style is usually the result of imbalanced rootage. In the process of exposing the root buttress during transplanting, it is not unusual to find roots that come out from the trunk a bit higher on one side than the roots on the opposite side. Achieve a balanced rootage in one of two ways. Graft on new roots all around the trunk at one level, or incline the trunk so roots are visible on the surface all around the trunk.

Inclining the trunk to expose a balanced rootage automatically creates a fine *shakan* style, but it is important to balance this *shakan* style or to stabilize it. One very nice way to stabilize this design is to position rocks in and among the exposed roots on your bonsai in order to make it appear as though the tree is not going to continue falling down. It must appear visually stable. Sometimes a series of walnut-sized rocks positioned in and among the roots during potting does just the trick in not only achieving the visual balanced rootage desirable for the *shakan* style, but also suggesting a certain rocky environmental condition wherein the tree is going to grasp the rocks and not continue to fall down.

During transplanting, simply insert some of these stones, rocks, or pebbles in and among the roots as they are exposed, to create a wonderful stable effect. In training branches, be aware that it is necessary to raise the branches on the down slant of the trunk in order to match the branches that are on the up side of the trunk. Always be aware that branches on the right and left side of a slanting style must be balanced with resepct to the horizontal.

Fig. 3-9. An extreme slanting wild Murrayana pine, **pinus contorta 'Murrayana'.**

PLACEMENT IN POT

Number One Branch

There is a great deal of discussion in the bonsai world about the placement of the bonsai in the bonsai container. As a general rule of thumb, the number one branch, which is the lowest, longest, and largest-diameter branch on the tree, needs the extra space in the container. If the number one branch is on the right-hand side, the bonsai is normally planted on the left-hand side of the container.

There are exceptions to this rule, of course, as there are exceptions to any rule. Ninety percent of the time, placing the number one branch on a slanting style over the bulk of the pot will position your tree to its best stylistic advantage. The other ten percent of the time, other considerations are important. I like to think of a tree as having a presentation. Looked at from its best location, straight toward the front, somewhere around the apex there is the appearance of inclination, almost as if the tree had a face. I have seen some trees where this inclination, or visual direction, is so strong that it overcomes the design need to position the number one branch over the bulk of the surface of the bonsai pot.

If, when you look at the front of the tree, this visual face, or presentation, is strong from right to left, it might look much better to plant this tree in the left-hand side of the pot so that the presentation goes over the bulk of the pot, in spite of the fact that the number one branch is on the left side of the tree. Conversely, it is possible, on about 10 percent of bonsai, to have a visual presentation in the top third of the tree that seems to orient itself from right to left. Trees such as this may be planted in the right-hand side of the bonsai container, in spite of the fact that the number one branch proceeds from the right-hand side of the tree. These are exceptions, but they are worthy of consideration.

Number Two Branch

Fig. 3-10 shows a Japanese maple that has all the typical design considerations one might expect of a slanting style. It has a strong number one branch on the right-hand side, a very weak number two branch on the left-hand side and a visual presentation toward the apex, as if the tree were looking to the right. All three of these aspects make it easy to plant this tree on the left-hand side of the container. If the number two branch is extremely strong, as it is in some trees, it may be necessary to take it into consideration

Fig. 3-10.

when placing the plant in the container. Again, it is important that the number two branch have the same inclination with respect to the horizontal as the number one branch, in order to achieve visual stability.

THE FOLIAGE TRIANGLE

As with all bonsai styles, the foliage triangle is important to the design of the tree. Please notice the natural tree in **fig. 3-11**. Note the prominent foliage triangle. The long horizontal number one branch is of course the major design feature of this *chu-shakan* tree. The number two branch on the opposite side is almost insignificant by comparison, but there is a very strong apex and the foliage triangle is distinct and quite clear. This tree obviously would be planted on the left side of the bonsai container.

Fig. 3-11.

In **fig. 3-12** this vine maple, *acer circinatum*, is a *sho-shakan* tree with a distinct foliage triangle as well. The number one branch is barely distinguishable from the number two branch. This is an extremely short, fat, and stubby old collected specimen and it was difficult when styling this tree to achieve a difference in visual height between the right- and left-hand sides. Actually, the number one branch is on the right-hand side and the number two branch proceeds just slightly higher from the trunk on the left hand side. The apex is generally rounded,

Fig. 3-12.

curved, and not very distinct; however, the overall impression of this tree is of a distinct foliage triangle. This tree is over 500 years old and it was difficult to place it either on the right-hand side or left-hand side of this pot because of its large trunk. Perhaps this was not significant because the number one branch did not dominate the number two branch; therefore, direction in the pot became less important.

WINDSWEPT

Although there is a design called the windswept style, the *shakan* style is often a fundamental beginning for what we call windswept. If you take a *shakan*-style tree and make the branches slightly longer on one side than on the other, it automatically becomes windswept style. The windswept style appears among *shakan* trees everywhere. **Fig. 3-13** shows the top of a tree that has died, creating a beautiful windswept *jin* on the coastline. Windswept trees from windy places such as the coast, or a gorge, or high mountainous regions with strong prevailing winds give inspiration for bonsai designs.

In **Fig. 3-14** there is wind within this rocky outcropping; however, the wind swirls because of the shapes of the surrounding rocks. Although there is a strong wind in this area all the time, the wind changes direction all the time, which is reflected in the branches of this tree. The branches are not smaller

Fig. 3-13.

Fig. 3-14.

excellent example of stability in this slanting style. The rootage is wedged in among these rocks, and notice the balance of the angle of the branches from right to left. This is a very good example of a number one and a number two branch proceeding from the trunk on the same side of the trunk. With extreme slanting styles such as this, notice how having these two branches proceed from the right-hand side tends to counterbalance the effect of the apex being so extremely far to the left on this tree. Proceeding up the trunk line, notice branches on the right and the left proceeding from the outsides of the curves, and notice that they have the same angle with respect to the horizontal on both the right- and left-hand sides of the trunk. There is a well defined apex, and it is easy to find the foliage triangle even though the number one and number two branches are both found on the right hand side of this tree.

Fig. 3-15.

ROOTAGE DISPLAY

The following two examples of bonsai illustrate the importance of visual rootage in the slanting style. In the Scotch pine, **fig. 3-16**, it was important to display the four surface roots below the encircling root which enclosed the tree just above. Without these surface roots, it would have been impossible to make this bonsai look stable. Imagine this particular tree with those lower visual roots covered up by soil. The large encircling root

on one side or the other, but they are sometimes smaller on one side, sometimes longer on the same side. On the opposite side is great variation as well. This has contributed to some of the undulations in the trunk as the tree tries to survive, slanting out from this rocky precipice.

By contrast, in **fig. 3-15** is an extreme slanting style, a *dai-shakan*, an

Fig. 3-16.

that comes toward the viewer would make it look as though the trunk were sitting on top of a rotating ball of roots. As an upright style of any kind, whether formal upright, *moyogi*, or *shakan*, it would have been impossible to give a sense of calm or stability to the viewer, but digging this soil level down just a few inches exposes some roots farther down.

Fig. 3-17 has a similar situation in a wild cherry. The problem with this tree is in the constricted trunk line just above where the old base of the roots was formerly located at the surface of the soil. Visualize this tree with the surface roots covered up with soil. The constriction would give the effect of a bottle inverted into sand. The top of the trunk would be larger than the bottom and the whole planting would have a very unstable appearance. This tree needed to incline slightly to one side as a *sho-shakan*, and needed to show that the trunk actually got larger down below. By scraping away soil down another five and a half inches below the trunk constriction, we are able to at-

tain visual stability. The root buttress in this tree becomes taller and the surface roots become part of the visual trunk.

In closing this chapter, I'd like to reiterate a couple of important points. It is extremely important to balance branches and rootage on both sides of the tree. In **fig. 3-18** the *jin* on this tree is imbalanced. The branches on the left side are stronger than the branches on the right. The angle of the branches on the left side is considerably farther below horizontal than the branches on the right side. The presence of various galls and swellings on this bonsai indicate a diseased planting. The presence of *jin* indicates that this tree is failing. The instability suggested by this slanting tree is unsettling.

In a bonsai, this would look like a dead tree that is about to fall down, and in fact, that's exactly what this tree is in nature. Learn from success in nature as well as failures. This particular tree is a tree that is part of nature, but it is about to become compost. I am sure you do not want your bonsai to look as if it is about to become part of this compost.

Fig. 3-17.

Fig. 3-18.

THE SEMI-CASCADE STYLE

Han Kengai

DESIGN CONSIDERATIONS

Discussing the stylistic merits of the *han kengai* style is difficult because so few examples of this style exist. I don't know whether it is the least popular style because it is difficult, or whether it is the least popular style because it is difficult to do well. When I study some of the examples of *han kengai*, many design peculiarities are revealed. For one, here is a pot that is about as tall as it is wide. In this container is not a totally upright tree, but a tree that has tried to go upright, but whose lowest number one branch is longer and lower.

From a design consideration, here is a half-cascade style, and indeed, *han kengai* translates as half cascade, or partial cascade. This style is difficult to achieve because it is unclear whether the semi-cascade style is going to end up being the finishing style or whether this is an intermediary style on the way to producing a full cascade. As in the full cascade style, here are trees that

Fig. 4-1.

display an apex that forms an individual bonsai in its own right. The top two-thirds of the tree resembles one of the upright styles. It could be a formal upright, but more often it is the *moyogi* or *shakan* style mentioned previously. What sets this style apart from the others is that the lowest branch, the

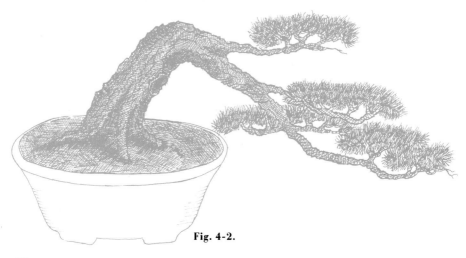

Fig. 4-2.

number one branch, is long and extends below the rim of the pot. Use a pot that is as tall as it is wide to accommodate the low reaching of this lowest branch.

In nature, there are different styles of semi-cascading tree. Illustration **4-1** shows a fine example of a high altitude tree that is having difficulty forming a strong apex because of ultraviolet light and snow load. The average snowfall in this area is heavy enough so that the apex is only exposed for about six months of the year. The lowest branches are exposed to the summer sun for only three months of the year by comparison. This forms a tree that is dominant in its lowest branches, because the lower branches are protected from frost. The upper branches are exposed to higher amounts of ultraviolet light, wind, increased desiccation, and overnight freezing temperatures, even in the summer. The lowest branches on this tree are really quite dominant and determine the style of this tree. This is classic semi-cascade style coming from nature.

In **fig. 4-3** a semi-cascade is formed at the edge of a rocky precipice or cliff. The calm lake below offers little respite for this tree that is struggling to grow from a little crack in the rock. No doubt this tree started its life as a seed that became lodged in the corner of this rocky shelf. As the tree struggled to grow, it first went up toward the light, but discovered that the roots were becoming confined in its natural rock container. As it grew, it used up available resources, and the resources that remained were directed toward where growth was easiest.

It is not difficult to imagine that when the wind picks up across this lake, the top of this tree is subjected to extreme wind forces and therefore desiccation of the new buds that form each year. The lowest branches on this tree will grow better and be healthier. They will grow longer and will have a greener growth as nutrient is redirected toward this fast-growing portion of the tree. In time, several unsuccessful tops will form from the top of the tree and down below, and branches will extend downward because they are protected close to the ground. Wind, as it passes across rocks, will have a certain amount of turbulence, but inside a rocky cliff or precipice next to a rocky wall, the wind has more difficulty gaining velocity. The swirling wind doesn't desiccate the plant as much as a straight blast across the lake toward the top of this tree.

Third, another semi-cascade style is on its way to becoming a full cascade style because of the nature of the plant material. In illustration **4-4** is a juniper, which has a tendency to hug the rocks for several reasons. First, it is a type of plant that weeps naturally because of its genetics. I suspect that over time this species developed this growth ability in order to survive. The weeping style not only enables this plant to grow in protected rocky crevasses, but it also helps it to keep close to the ground where wind velocity is low and moisture from the ground is close at hand. An added benefit of this growth style is that the tree can root itself

Fig. 4-3.

Fig. 4-4.

along its lowest branches in order to provide additional nutrition and moisture from these advantageous roots.

Coming across trees like this in the woods, it's possible to pick up a low branch and notice that it is rooted into the ground in several places. Many landscape materials exhibit this same tendency. The lower branches of rhododendrons and azaleas, when covered with soil, will root themselves. Many weeping or prostrate-type junipers will also root themselves. The illustration above is a common juniper, found in the western Cascades. If the lowest branches come across a moist area of humus, they will root into this area, and these new secondary, or advantageous, roots can help supply nutrition for the plant as a whole. As stated earlier, portions of this plant are the *han kengai* style. Other portions of the same plant could be regarded as the full-cascading style, depending on how far the plant has dropped over the edge of a rock. In bonsai terms, the height of the container itself would determine whether this plant is truly a *han kengai* or a *kengai* style.

FORMAL *HAN KENGAI*

In **fig. 4-5**, a number of plants are growing next to a rocky ledge in a windy area. Some of the plants around have actively growing tops, others in this area have dead tops. Some have

portions of tops which have died and new tops that have tried to take over where this top *jin* was formed. The formal *han kengai* takes these various degrees of desiccation into account. The name "formal" merely signifies that this is an upright growing tree and that there is some semblance of an apex, whether it is live or not.

In **fig. 4-6** is another example of a tree that has an excellent *han kengai* shape. This is in a lowland area, obviously with plenty of moisture. You can see the waterfall easily in the background and a stream running by. This woodland glade is about 1,000 feet (300 m) in altitude, and gets about

Fig. 4-5.

Fig. 4-6.

30–40 inches (75–100 cm) of rainfall per year. The tree is struggling only because it is in the rocky crevice.

If it were growing in the woods below, it would grow up to be a magnificent formal upright. But instead, the tree is forced to grow in this natural container at the edge of a rocky ledge, and in spite of the moisture and nutrition available, the tree struggles. The top is green, although it is short. The bottom branches are reaching out toward the moisture and reaching out toward the protection against the cliff. This gives a good study in the elements found in a good formal *han kengai* style. Notice that the apex is moving in the same direction as the tip of the lowest branch. This is typical of most cascading styles. If the lowest branches of this tree were removed and only the top half of the tree were studied, it would form the typical foliage triangle found in the upright styles mentioned in the first three chapters of this book.

In **fig. 4-7** is another puzzling style of bonsai. This tree illustrates several of the points that are important when designing *han kengai* style. The pot is fairly tall, as compared with most bonsai containers, but it is not as wide as it is tall. The lowest branch certainly extends below the rim of the pot, which would indicate this to be a semicascade style, yet the strong apex, which rises considerably above the pot, would indicate that the dominant branches are not, in fact, the lower branches.

This is a puzzling situation because, due to snow load, this tree gradually became a weeping pine. This type of pine, which is a lodgepole pine, normally grows in quite an upright fashion. This tree was growing at such a high altitude that the top was consistently nipped away by frost. Every spring, it tried to put out some new growth. Protected down in the snow below, the new buds thrived and have grown into this unusual weeping style. The lowest live branch on this tree actually proceeds from the top of the

Fig. 4-7.

tree. It's not entirely as it appears: the number one branch is actually dead and is covered by foliage that comes from the top of the tree. The number one branch is only maintained as a *shari* element on the tree.

INFORMAL *HAN KENGAI*

This variety of semi-cascade style begins by having no top, no apex whatsoever. Often this may be a weeping type of tree, similar to that in **fig. 4-3** above. Or this could be a tree that is living under such stressful conditions that new tops were nipped very early while they were still sensitive buds, and a portion of woody apex, even dead *jin*, simply did not form. Sometimes the tops of these weeping cascades are really quite polished with sand and sleet, wind forces and the bleaching of high amounts of ultraviolet light.

This is perhaps the most difficult style to accomplish of all the styles that I know in bonsai. It is extremely difficult to present to the viewer a style that feels comfortable. By comfortable, I mean that the tree looks as though it has lasted already for a very long time and will last well into the future. A bonsai style that appears transient is very unsettling to view. Imagine a tree that looks as if it is falling out of the pot rather than leaning over by its own choice. It looks as though gravity is taking over. Perhaps it looks as if there is a great deal of erosion on the roots. The whole tree looks very unsettling and not very appealing by comparison to other stately trees. I think, for this reason, the semi-cascade without an apex is difficult to do. The task of the designer is to exaggerate stable rootage by using rocks to make it appear as though this tree has been growing in rocky soil and is actually quite stable. Try to make the long, lowest branch look like an important part of the tree; make it look as though the tree not only has been there a long time, but will survive for many centuries to come.

Fig. 4-9. Some examples of semi-cascade containers.

Fig. 4-8. A semi-cascade golden threadbranch cypress, **chamaecyparis pisifera filifera** *'aurea'.*

THE CONTAINERS

The semi-cascade container is approximately as high as it is wide. Many are the opportunities for color and texture and style. Round pots are available. The potter's wheel works very well to make a semi-cascade pot. Just have a basic vase shape. Sometimes the top edge is flared out; sometimes it is flared in; sometimes the pot is straight up and down. Embellish the sides with various lines of texture. The middle of the pot can swell out. There are a number of shapes available in these round pots. They are the most efficient pot in terms of the amount of volume they

hold. Volume relates to root mass that can be included within the bonsai container and resistance to drying out.

Sometimes the semi-cascade pot is made square, almost looking like a cube, with the top portion of the cube open to receive the tree. Some prefer to align the pot so the flat side of this cube is seen from the front. Others prefer to view the bonsai straight toward one of the corners. Most people prefer looking at the flat side, but it is perfectly fine in a show to align the tree so the viewer is looking toward one corner of the square.

One of the advantages I can see for looking at the corner of the square pot is that often the number one branch is not going straight to the right side or straight to the left side, but has movement toward the viewer. By aligning the corner of the pot toward the viewer, you are allowing a bit more room for this number one branch to drape over the side of the pot. It doesn't have to drape over the corner of the pot, in other words. The number one branch would then come across one of the flat sides of the container. Some square containers have very high legs. There is a popular cloud-shaped leg that raises the square pot up fairly high, almost like one of the literati-style containers found later in this book. Obviously there are other styles as well.

When you look at the semi-cascade pot from above, sometimes you see hexagonal containers or octagonal containers. In these cases, it is permissible to view one of the corners of the hexagonal pot, but in the case of the octagonal pot, you are always looking straight at one of the flat sides. Legs may be tall or there may be no legs at all, but oftentimes there is some indication of elevation, in order to take the drain hole up off the bonsai bench. This allows greater air circulation and increased oxygen to the roots.

In the hexagon or the octagon, make sure that you are happy with the positioning of the legs of the container. It is all too easy to transplant or pot a bonsai into a round, hexagonal, or octagonal container without regard to the legs below, because the tendency is to pot looking down at the top of the pot. You won't notice that the legs are not in proper position until you put it up on the bonsai stand after repotting, and then it is difficult to move the tree.

Fig. 4-10 shows another species of juniper that has a tendency to grow faster horizontally than vertically. The genetics of this plant allow it to drape over rocks when it is necessary to hug close to the rock, but it can reach across large spaces between rocks as well, and it does form a fairly nice apex. In planting this as a semi-

cascade style, we just simply take the lowest branch and extend it over the edge of a container that is about as wide as it is tall, and allow the branch to weep down. If you can imagine the finished planting on your bonsai bench, this weeping branch should proceed in a horizontal fashion, slightly toward the viewer, and the weeping tip of the branch not come as far down as the lowest portion of your pot. The green tip of this branch should end somewhere between the top of the container and the bottom of the container, off to the right, or off to the left of the planting. If it weeps any farther than that, it might be necessary to put your plant in a much taller container, at which point it would become a weeping, full-cascade style.

ROOTAGE

Fig. 4-11 shows a spectacular example of rootage on a semi-cascade tree. This is not only a rugged area, but the little rocky crevice that the seed was originally lodged in was insufficient to support this tree, and as you can see from

Fig. 4-10.

Fig. 4-11.

the undulations of the trunk, it has tried desperately to get out of this container and to root itself in other places in order to survive. This is a fine example of a tree that will form a trunk as it seeks moisture. Notice the strong rootage below the root buttress, and notice all the *jin*, *shari*, and *saba miki* toward the south side of this tree, where high amounts of ultraviolet light have totally desiccated it.

This semi-cascade style is therefore created by the plant trying to grow toward the south, toward the drying winds and drying sun and the extreme snow load in this area. Where there is wind, there is also danger of dessication due to frost. The successful branches grow closer to the ground, where they are protected by snowfall. At an altitude of 5,000 feet (1500 m), it is impossible for upper branches to become very tall, not so much because of the frost, but because of the limited resources of growing in this natural, rocky container.

In designing a semi-cascade style as bonsai, make sure not only that you do have an interesting root buttress that is wide, but that this buttress extends out even wider unto visible surface roots on both sides of the tree. If possible, locate your largest roots on the sunny side of this tree—in other words, on the opposite side from your number one branch. The number one branch in nature is going to cool the ground comparatively. In the above illustration, note how the stronger roots are on the sunny, or south, side of this tree. This functions for strength as well, and is caused by the sun and the heat concentrating in the soil. A combination of this heat and moisture will cause roots to grow just a tiny bit faster on that side of the tree than they do on the other side of the tree. It functions visually, because the tree appears more stable, with larger roots on the weak side of the tree, away from the weight of the branches. The exposed rootage molds itself well into a tall container, and it is beautiful to see these tall, curving roots gripping this tree inside a semi-cascade container. It gives the planting stability.

SIZE OF BRANCHES

As in all the previous styles, these adhere to the principle that the number one branch should be the longest and the lowest. With the cascading-type styles, this is most important, because it is the primary design element. It is the part that defines the cascade. Avoid at all times trying to cascade the top of your tree. I've seen beginners take a juniper and, after placing the roots in the pot, wire the top of the tree down, in order to attempt a semi-cascade style. This contributes to the instability of this style, because the top of the tree looks as though it were failing. This is a planting that appears unlikely to succeed. Instead, try to think of the top two-thirds of the bonsai as an upright style, perhaps a *moyogi* style, perhaps *shakkan*.

When treating the top of the tree as an upright style, the result is a feeling of stability and balance. The number one branch simply becomes exaggerated. Allow it to grow over time. If the tip of the branch extends just below the rim of a pot, a semi-cascade pot will give a semi-cascade bonsai design. If over time you are able to extend or divide and redivide this number one branch into other branchlets, you create the full cascading style. Bonsai literature displays semi-cascade trees that grew lushly, with lower branches that became so large that the bonsai was styled slightly differently, tipped at just slightly a different angle and planted in a tall pot, making a semi-cascade tree into a full cascade.

Always keep in mind the ratio of height to width of a tree. You will discover, as you try to design bonsai, that a tree that is just as high as it is wide looks a bit more boring than a tree that is wider than it is tall or taller than it is wide. With a semi-cascade style, remember, the long, lowest number one branch has a tendency to make the total bonsai design wider than it is tall. This is good. Do not allow your apex to become too strong or too tall. The apex should look like a small version of an upright tree, but it should remain secondary. It should not be the primary focus of the semi-cascade style. The part which makes the semi-cascade dramatic is the horizontal drop of the number one branch. Keep these proportions in mind as you maintain your tree.

RECOMMENDED SPECIES

Any plant that has a tendency to grow slightly wider than it is tall is a natural for this type of design. In considering species to use for this style, consider the natural shape of older trees. A maple often will grow about as wide as it is tall. Others will grow really quite short and stout, like the English hedge maple. Within species itself, there is quite a variety of genetic difference. We can take advantage of some of these genetic differences to create the semi-cascade style. Some pines grow quite upright, and always stay fairly cylindrical. Ponderosa pines and lodgepole pines often grow this way naturally, with a tall spike up at the top, and a flame shape outline as they mature. There are, by contrast, varieties of the Swiss mountain pine, Italian stone pine, or mugho pine that grow much wider than they are tall, and these varieties of pine are more suitable to the cascade or semi-cascade style. As you go through this list of species, keep in mind that the variety within the species is perhaps more important than the species itself.

Abies, acer, andromeda, aralia, arbutus, arctostaphylus, aucuba, azalea, berberis, bougainvillea, buxus, camellia, cercis, chaemacyparis, coffea, cornus, corokia, cotoneaster, crab apple, daphne, erica, ficus, gardenia, juniperus, kalmia, malus, nandina, olea, parrotia, photinia, physocarpus, pieris, pinus, pistachia, plum, prune, pyracantha, pyrus, quercus, rhododendron, rosa, serrisa, taxus, ulmus, wisteria, and zelkova.

THE CASCADE STYLE
Kengai

GENERAL CONSIDERATIONS

Perhaps one of the most unusual and most dramatic styles of the bonsai world is the cascade style. It is highly unusual to see trees draping over the sides of pots, but these styles come from unusual trees in nature. They get their inspiration from the mountains, the coasts, and gorges. They occur in some of the most extreme micro-environments known to plant life. For those who grew up in flatter areas of the country, it is harder to imagine some of these trees. **Fig. 5-1** shows a magnificent example of a juniper cascading from a rock crevasse in the side of a rocky ravine. The branches are swept downward, and yet the growth tips continue to reach for the sun to survive. This is a beautiful example of the cascading plant in nature.

Fig. 5-1.

or top. Instead, due to the ground effect, the wind is unable to have as much of an influence on a plant the closer it gets to the soil surface. A 50 mile (80 km) an hour wind at 10 feet (3 m) above the soil surface may be reduced to as much as 10 miles (16 km) per hour on average, within a foot (30 cm) of the ground. The plant can feel this lack of wind and it responds to the decreased amount of desiccation toward the ground by putting out larger, lower branches at high altitudes and in gorges and when it is trying to grow on the edge of a cliff. This naturally leads to the production of not only long lower branches, but heavily weighted lower branches, which have a tendency to plummet over the edges of precipices.

The Alpine Lowering of Branches

In the case of this plant at a high altitude, the juniper is forced to grow downward because of the tremendous weight of snow in the winter. Snow remains on this plant from September through June the following year. Only in late June is this plant exposed to sunlight and allowed to grow. You can see the important influence of this weight of snow on the shape of this plant over a rock. Every time a new branch attempts to come out in a horizontal fashion, the weight of the snow will pull this juniper down and give it its present shape. Notice the shape of the trunk, the direction of the trunk, the root stability, and the presence of *jin* and *shari* on this plant. All of these design features contribute to the effect of great age and beauty.

The Wind Favoring Lower Branches

As was mentioned in the discussion on the semi-cascade style, it is well known that a tree that grows in a very windy place tends to have a very weak apex,

The Natural Genetic Weeping of Plants

Fig. 5-2 shows a natural juniper planting at low altitude. This type of juniper is a prostrate, or horizontal, juniper. Through genetic selection, plants in areas of lower elevation are able to re-root themselves along the surfaces of soil to gain advantage over other plants in the same area. These plants are beautiful and they create a most striking display. The illustration above represents to the bonsai designer a natural shape that can be used in the bonsai container. Not only is a plant like this good material for the cascading plant, it is excellent for more upright varieties of bonsai called the weeping style. One can almost imagine the container on

Fig. 5-2.

the left side of the illustration above, and what a gorgeous bonsai this would be in terms of fluidity of design and natural grace and harmony with the container. In its present state in nature, the rock crevice itself is the container, and the rocks around it form the sides of the pot. You can see the harmony of color between the rocks and the striking green foliage as it flows from left to right in a combination of cascading and weeping style, associated with this type of juniper.

THE FORMAL CASCADE

The Apex

Perhaps the most striking differentiation between the formal cascade and the informal cascade, which follows, is the presence of an apex. Not only is the apex upright, it is directional as well. The apex, after all, experiences the same direction of wind the rest of the plant does, only more so. It is the direction of the apex that determines the direction of the number one branch. Therefore, when designing a formal cascade bonsai, please appreciate this design from nature. If a large number one branch is hanging as far as it does, it is natural to assume that the forces above must have been going in that very same direction; otherwise, the number one branch would not exist at all. It does not make much design sense to have the apex of a formal cascade bonsai going in the opposite direction of the number one branch.

The Foliage Triangle

If you were to isolate the top half of the tree on your formal cascade bonsai, you should be able to see a smaller, upright bonsai form. Let's imagine removing the number one branch and the number two branch of a formal cascade bonsai. In a technical sense, though not an exact one, the number three branch, then, would become the

number one branch of the top half of the tree. Imagine for just a minute the number three branch on this tree as the number one branch of the top of your formal cascade style. Look your design over carefully. Have you created a smaller version of the larger tree in the top half of your cascading design? If you have, you have a very pleasing design indeed. All the branch forms present in a typical upright form, such as the *moyogi* style or the *shakkan* style, are present in the top half of a successful cascading plant. The individual foliage triangle is still there, as is the separation of the branches from larger at the base to smaller approaching the apex. In other words, closer to the top of tree the branches become shorter, closer, and so compact the trunk at the top of the tree is not visible.

Total Tree Foliage Triangle

Above, the consideration was the foliage triangle in the top half of the tree. Now, consider the foliage triangle for a cascading bonsai. Consider the tip of the number one branch as one point, the tip of the number two branch as the second point, and the tip of the apex as the third point in this imaginary triangle. Notice that it is still a triangle and that the triangle is extremely elongated as compared with any of the other bonsai styles, yet that it is still a triangle and still something to be considered when designing a tree.

The Relationship of Trunk to Branch

As with all other styles, the number one branch is the thickest branch, the longest branch, the lowest branch, and the branch that contains the most foliage mass. Proceeding in the trunk from lowest to highest, each branch duplicates the number one branch until the top third of the foliage triangle, at which point it becomes less important and, in fact, the individual branches become indiscernible. At that point a crown toward the apex is formed, where the trunk is not visible at all. In most upright styles, this is quite obvious and very easy to design. In the formal cascade it is often ignored, to the detriment of the design of the plant. Too often, a person will try to create a formal cascade by taking a pine or juniper, planting it in a pot, and swinging the largest part of the plant toward the ground. To compensate for this poor design, the beginner will try to turn up a branch to make it appear that this branch always was the apex of the tree. The design is poor, and the effect fails, because the bonsai grower has failed to grasp how the cascade tree really grows. When you consider the cascading tree in nature, the oldest part of the tree is still the trunk. The oldest part of the tree is not the number one branch, and when you look at poor design, this is often the cause of this visual uncertainty.

Consider **fig. 5-3**. Notice how the number one branch is the longest; it contains the most foliage; it's the lowest on the tree; and it sweeps down below the bottom of this extremely tall bonsai top. Notice in particular the number of branchlets that come off this number one branch. These branchlets function as different clouds of foliage to layer out this tree so it starts duplicating what happens in nature. Refer back to fig. 5-1 for a moment and compare fig. 5-1 with this bonsai, fig. 5-3. Notice the similarity. They're both junipers. They both sweep downward, and the largest, longest, and lowest branches are turned up, always fighting against gravity, to form these small branchlets. If you copy this style, you are bound to produce a pleasing bonsai.

THE INFORMAL CASCADE

Once in a while, while walking through the woods, I come across a magnificent example of one of the bonsai styles. The tree in **fig. 5-4** is one of these incredible natural bonsais. This trunk epitomizes the informal cascade. Notice a lack of apex. It's hard to describe this tree, and, indeed, it is even difficult to photograph it, because the tree proceeds from the top of a rocky ledge that is very difficult to climb. I was only able to photograph the root buttress and the downward curve of this pine by climbing up and taking this picture with a wide-angle lens.

The tree is magnificent from all angles, but it is difficult to get a good photograph of it as this beautiful pine tree plummets down over this 1,000 foot (300 m) rocky ledge. It is a magnificent example of the natural, informal cascade in nature. Its lack of apex is not disturbing. Notice the fine texture of the bark and the direction and the smoothness of the trunk. This trunk does not look weak. It does not look as if it is wilting. It looks as though it has been here for a thousand years, and will continue to be here for a thousand years more. The presence of these huge boulders creates an effect of stability. The rock is the container itself—a 1,000-foot (300 m) -high cascading pot. The empty space inside this crevasse is where the soil and the roots are contained, just as we would

Fig. 5-3.

Fig. 5-4.

do in bonsai. Down below, the branches sweep toward the ground because of winter snow at 3,000 feet (900 m) in elevation. More important, they turn upwards on the tips as if to challenge this force.

The informal cascade can be characterized mainly by its lack of style and lack of rules, but one point cannot be ignored—that an informal cascade without an apex must have a good stable root buttress, must have a good exposed root spread that is visible easily to the eye, must have a very stable, strong-looking container in earth tones, and must have the growing tips trying to reach back up toward the light. If you can duplicate these design features on your bonsai, it will succeed.

Fig. 5-5.

Consider the informal upright cascade in **fig. 5-5**. There is no apex on this tree. There is a high point of the tree, but it is technically not an apex, because it is just simply the height of a downward-curving trunk. The trunk of this juniper is huge. The tree is perhaps 350 years old. This is a common juniper, *juniperus communis*, which has been grafted with *shimpaku* juniper. The new apex, which is struggling to come back up again, is still below the dip of the original *shari*. There is no particular design to this, and I can't explain why I like it, except to say that I like the diameter of the trunk. I like the twigginess of the *jin*, *shari* and *saba miki* over the entire length of the tree, and I like the vigor of the new *shimpaku* branches as they are leaning up toward the light. In spite of the fact that this trunk line is coming up from the pot and is bent downward, the overall effect is of stability.

THE CONTAINER

Height

Perhaps the most obvious feature of a bonsai container that will house a cascading style is the height of the container itself. If you come across a container that is considerably higher than it is wide, it is called a cascading pot. The cascading pot is designed to accommodate the long, low-reaching number one branch. It is very ineffective to plant one of the upright styles in a cascading pot. The effect is imbalanced and unstable. If the number one branch is hanging over the edge of the pot and it is reaching up toward the light, as if to recover, there is a sense of harmony with the container. Remember, whenever you see bonsai containers that are considerably higher than they are wide, these are designed for the cascading style.

Proportion and Shape

Cascade pots have a tremendous amount of volume inside the container. Plants remain healthy for a couple of reasons. First, because of this tremendous volume, water retention is great, and second, because of the shape of the container, excess water is instantly removed because of the forces of gravity. A good bonsai soil that has been screened is highly granular and will not allow any excess water to remain inside the container. The hardest containers to have good drainage are the very flat *saikei* trays, or landscape trays. These trays may be two, three, or four feet (60, 90, or 120 cm) long, and only an inch (2.5 cm) high. It is very difficult for them to drain very well.

At first, this doesn't seem to make sense, but consider a ktichen sponge. Take a kitchen sponge soaked in water, lay it down flat on the kitchen counter, and two hours later it will still be wet. Take another kitchen sponge, lay it down on its edge on the same kitchen counter, and two hours later it will be dry. The same principle is true of bonsai pots. The taller the bonsai pot, the more apt it is to drain well. Taller pots and round pots the shape of cascading pots have a tendency to hold more volume of soil compared with shallow pots. It is very easy to keep cascading bonsai alive because even poor soil drains well.

To determine the size and shape of a cascading pot for your bonsai, I would recommend that you style your tree initially in the nursery container and then make sure you are taking into consideration the height of the tree as well as the length of the number one branch. If the length of the number one branch is two feet, then a cascading pot which is slightly less than two feet (60 cm) will be just about right for a new bonsai plant. Consider the size of the nursery container it came from. If you started with a three gallon (11 liter) nursery container, which is about eight inches (20 cm) across, then consider getting a cascading pot that is about six inches (15 cm) across.

Consider also the exposed roots that you will need to display on the surface of your bonsai soil. Make sure there is adequate diameter in your cascading pot to display these roots properly. It does not look particularly stable to curve your exposed roots down and jam them into a bonsai container. More properly, the roots should have a natural curvature, or shape, that does not come to the edges of the container. This gives a more natural feeling to the tree and gives it a feeling of stability without giving the impression that the pot is controlling the roots; rather, it is the roots naturally curving down and making that shape on the soil surface.

Color

As with all bonsai containers, it is helpful to consider the earth-brown, gray, and dull glazes for the conifers.

Fig. 5-6. A very old cascading juniper graft, juniperus horizontalis *'communis', showing its large bent trunk, jin, and complex descending first branch.*

Brighter-colored glazes look best with fruiting and flowering plants. It is possible, for example, that if you have a cascading cotoneaster, it will have white flowers and red berries, and some fall color in the leaves as well. A cascading pot of dark cobalt blue will look nice with the color of the red berries, the orange foliage, and the white flowers as well. Try not to duplicate the color of the flower in the color of the pot. A cascading pink azalea looks quite garish in a cascading pink pot.

Position of Legs

As with all cascading pots, full cascading pots as well as semi-cascading pots, there is quite a variety of round pots, square pots, hexagonal pots, and octagons. There are pots that are partially square and have rounded corners. There are pots that have carved windows or calligraphy. Most important is the position of the legs in the bottom of a pot. It is usually uncomfortable to position one leg toward the viewer, and while you are transplanting, replanting, or styling your tree, make sure you are aware of the position of the legs in that pot. It is all too easy to transplant from a nursery container into a cascading pot without reference to those legs, simply because you are working from above during this process.

On several types of pot, you may find it unpleasant that the legs are a very bright color. With stoneware, the color of the clay is always the color of the legs, regardless of the glaze, or lack of glaze. With porcelain, however, or with lighter colors of clay, it is possible to have a deep, rich brown or black pot that has a very bright, cream-colored leg. A permanent, indelible pen will darken this garish color quite easily and it will remain dark for a very long time. After a few years, the leg may need to be touched up with a pen again, but it does remove that bright element in an otherwise pleasantly dark planting.

THE STAND

I have temporarily positioned this fir bonsai, **fig. 5-7**, on this cherry stand. This relationship illustrates a few points that are worthy of discussion.

Fig. 5-7.

Display

On all bonsai, including the cascade styles, there is an imaginary point halfway from the bottom of the tree to the top of the tree. This is known as the visual point. If this visual point is maintained at eye level during styling and display, the designer can assure viewers that they are seeing the design that was meant to be communicated. In the illustration above, the viewing point is positioned at about eye level on the bonsai shelf. The bonsai shelf is 44 inches (112 cm) in height. My eye level tends to be just above five feet (150 cm) in height; therefore, the stand that I need for this plant has to be about a foot (30 cm) high. Choose your stands for each cascading tree that you have. They are easily constructed and they can be modified after purchase if necessary, but it is important in a show that your cascading plant display its visual point at eye level for most viewers. In Japan, I noticed that most bonsai shelves were about 40 inches

(100 cm) from the ground. On average, this will produce a pleasing show where the viewers aren't constantly rocking up and down on their toes or ducking their heads down to view the bonsai in its best presentation and form.

Proportion

Note that the top of this stand is slightly larger than the base of the container. If the stand is considerably larger, it has a tendency to dwarf the container and diminish the importance of the tree. If the stand is too small, it gives a feeling of instability and the tree looks as though it's about to fall over. The size of the legs should not detract from the diameter of the trunk. A cascading-type display stand should have a fairly thin leg. Larger legs distract the eye from the tree. People will notice the stand and the tree will look insignificant by comparison. By contrast, a stand that looks strong, is well built, and is put together by using narrow bits of wood adds importance and weight to the bonsai and is far more pleasing.

Fig. 5-8. An arrangement of forest-style maple, slanting-style juniper, and a tall cascading Japanese green mound juniper, **juniperus chinensis procumbens 'nana'.**

Design

Try to select a stand that is not overly garish. In most cases, the cascading plant is a conifer that is going to be fairly plain, and the pot will be a dull earth-tone color, and so the stand should be simple in structure and in color. Bright colors of wood detract from such plain trees. Avoid blonde wood, bleached wood, and reddish stains. Avoid intense finishes that are too shiny. It is very distracting to have a gorgeous stand with a very plain tree on top. The type of wood selected is sometimes quite important. A brilliantly colored redwood stand would be really quite distracting underneath a redwood tree.

KENGAI IN OTHER FORMS

Weeping

As has been shown in some of the illustrations above, it is possible to have *kengai* in weeping forms. What is perhaps less obvious is that upright forms that are weeping can develop into cascading forms, only because the length of the branches has increased so much, it is necessary to plant the bonsai in a taller container. I have many trees that started out as slanting, or *moyogi*, bonsai that were made from genetically weeping plants, such as the golden thread branch cypress, or the juniper procumbens nana. As the long, weeping branches stretched down, it seemed a shame to cut them off. Rather than cut off the branches, I simply transferred these plants from a shallow container to a slightly taller container. As the branches continued to develop, I enjoyed them very much, and these plants eventually became a semi-cascade and then finally a full cascade style. It is not always necessary to have a cascading-style trunk in order to have a cascading-style bonsai. Sometimes the cascading-style pots can be used for effective weeping-style bonsai as well.

Rock Planting

It is quite possible that when you plant a tree on top of a rock, the lower branches of your bonsai will start to lean down. Under these conditions, what started out as an upright rock planting may gradually turn into a cascading plant, just as plants do in nature. I think this is a nice concept: that you can plant an upright-style plant on top of a rock and have it gradually turn into a cascade-style tree, just the way it happens in nature. The top of the plant grows more slowly because rock plantings are generally more difficult to water and maintain. The lower branches of your bonsai start hugging the rock, and they fare better than the upper branches. It is quite possible over time to create a cascading rock planting that follows the very same processes that happen in nature.

Saikei

With miniature landscapes, it is possible to plant a number of trees around or on top of rocks, in order to create the effect of a seashore, a gorge, or rock planting, such as *p'en j'ing*. When these plants start to grow and mature, they have a tendency to have a mind of their own. The lower branches will creep toward moisture and shade. The upper branches have a tendency to grow more slowly because of sunlight. I have found it fascinating to see some of my larger group plantings, rock plantings, and *saikei* form natural shapes without pruning. I have long felt that bonsai should copy nature, and I find it extremely gratifying that miniature landscapes in containers conform to the very stresses in nature that I was trying to duplicate when I put the planting together in the first place. Established *saikei* will form their own shapes. One year, I noticed that a seedling had sprouted at the base of a tree that I was trying to grow. The seedling had sprouted from a seed from the parent plant that I was trying

Fig. 5-9. A young cascading mugho pine, **pinus mugho mughus.**

to grow. The parent plant died, but the seedling survived and it made a very interesting natural effect. We see these sorts of forces in nature, and I think they should have a profound influence on our design of *saikei*.

SUGGESTED PLANT MATERIAL

In the previous chapter, I mentioned a number of species that lend themselves well to the cascading style. The species recommended for the semi-cascade style are certainly recommended for the full-cascade style, *kengai*, as well. Here, by common name, are some of the plants used regularly to make cascading bonsai.

The nest spruce, English hedge maple, dwarf andromeda, satsuki azalea, Arctic birch, bougainvillea, Japanese camellia, weeping Atlantic cedar, flowering quince, thread branch cypress, chrysanthemum, corokia cotoneaster, Isis fuchsia, gardenia, various forms of ivy, green carpet juniper, Japanese green mound juniper, dwarf Japanese pieris, mugho pine, pyracantha, creeping Jenny, rhododendron, weeping Canadian hemlock, and Japanese wisteria.

GROWING METHODS

It may surprise the reader to notice the inclusion of chrysanthemum in the above list of plant material suitable for the full cascading bonsai style. Chrysanthemum is an important historical plant in Japan. The imperial throne of Japan is known as the chrysanthemum throne, and the chrysanthemum used to be a plant grown by the royal family exclusively. In recent times, the chrysanthemum has been revered for its symbolism and historical past. Many fine bonsai are made from chrysanthemums for this reason. The Japanese, in an attempt to include the chrysanthemum as a cascading bonsai, developed an unusual technique.

Some trees can be trained by being grown on their side. Various modifications to this procedure can be designed by the grower. Sometimes I grow a cascade plant on its side in order to develop a strong number one branch. Sometimes I grow it on its side in order to prevent the pot from being tipped over by squirrels or blue jays. But, more important, it gives a way of understanding plant hormones and how these hormones affect the direction of growth in a plant.

It is possible, for example, to take a strong upright tree, such as a Japanese maple, and turn it into a fine cascading plant, simply by growing it on one side. Various methods can be employed to achieve this end. The easiest is simply to have two pots for the bonsai. One pot is the training pot and the other is for display purposes only. They are both the same size, except that the opening for the plant root ball is on the side of the training container and the plant is grown on its side. The display pot is a typical cascade pot in which the root ball is simply put down into the end of this container and put upright so that the top of the tree becomes the number one branch. Again, refer to the illustration in this section to understand this procedure.

It is possible to use gravity to influence and train your plants. It is also possible to use light direction to orient new growth. This type of training technique simply uses the forces that guide the plant upward to produce a plant whose primary strength is directed downward. I have even grown bonsai upside down. All you have to do is make a training pot where the bonsai plant can be inserted through the drain holes in the container, and you have a container that will grow the pot in a completely inverted position. Instead of wiring the branches down, we use the plant's ability to force upward growth, to force an eventual alpine effect, once the tree is inverted.

Some trees can be trained entirely without wire. An Alberta spruce is normally quite apically dominant. All branches and all new growth want to grow upward in a very strong fashion. I found the Alberta spruce to be an extremely frustrating plant to grow as a formal upright tree, but I found if I grew this tree upside down, I could use this strong growth to produce horizontal growth.

The same principles hold true for designing and training cascading bonsai. Everyone knows what happens when a nursery container falls on its side and is not picked up for some time. The trunk will curve toward the light and up away from the earth, creating a curve in the trunk. Use these techniques to design bonsai and train trunks and branches without wire, clamps, or turnbuckles. With some engineering, I suspect that most bonsai material could be suitable for the cascading styles. Let your imagination be your guide, and good luck with your horticultural experimentation.

THE WINDSWEPT STYLE
Fukinagashi

DESIGN CONSIDERATIONS

The windswept style is the first style we have considered thus far that is not a member of the big five styles in bonsai. It is possible to style a windswept style by using any of the previous angles of inclination. For example, you may have a windswept tree that has a perfectly straight trunk, similar to the formal upright. Often windswept trees are slanted or have curving trunks, however. And, although it is rare, it is possible to have windswept trees that are semi-cascade or even full cascade in a gorge situation. The angle of the trunk becomes important as a design consideration. By noticing the relative length of branches from one side to the other, you can determine the extent of the wind that is subjecting a tree to stress. If the wind, for example, is moving from left to right, obviously the branches are going to be longer on the right-hand side of the tree. Observe a bonsai with branches only on the right-hand side of the tree, and it's easy to assume that it's an attempt at a style suggesting a tree in nature subjected to extreme winds at all times. On the other hand, a bonsai with branches only slightly larger on the right-hand side than the left suggests a bit of prevailing wind, but that sometimes the wind stops.

Extent of Wind

The extent to which the wind affects the size, shape, texture, and fullness of the branches depends on a number of factors. Obviously, the speed of the wind is most important. But consider as well the relative humidity in the area. If a tree is subject to an average 30 mile (50 km) an hour wind from left to right, and is at the coast, it will be under less stress than a similar tree in the desert. Hot, dry winds moving over a tree are far more damaging to a tree's design than cool, wet winds on the coast. Temperature plays an important part. Go into the high desert or up to the mountains, and notice the immediate rise in heat—not so much because of the actual temperature, but because of the effect the sun has on our skin. Even winter skiers wear considerable amounts of sunblock, because at higher altitudes the intensity of ultraviolet light is considerably greater than at sea level. Trees feel this as well. A 70°F (20°C) day in the mountains is far more desiccating than a 70°F (20°C) day at the beach.

Fig. 6-1. This young lodgepole pine, pinus contorta, *is developing long branches on the right. This is the first stage of developing a windswept-style bonsai.*

Another factor that influences the shape of the tree is how often the wind blows. I have lived in areas of the country where the wind seemed to pick up at four o'clock in the afternoon, but at dusk would settle down to almost a standstill. In rocky areas and gorges and in high desert rim rock, it is possible that the trees are subject to extreme winds at some times and almost no wind at other times. In such terrains, with frequent ups and downs in the landscape, the constancy of wind is far more difficult to predict and far more difficult to express in design. With a tree that is hanging over a rocky ledge, it is possible that the prevailing wind will come from one direction. Because of rocks and other trees, the wind has a tendency to swirl. Very short trees experience the natural drag of the wind as it rolls along the ground at a much slower speed than just a few feet off the ground.

The previous chapter talked about the length of branches and their success and failure in dealing with this natural slowing of air toward the ground level. Designing a bonsai to have considerably longer branches at the base of the trunk and quickly coming up to an embattled apex sends a message to the viewer that this tree is growing in an area where wind turbulence allows the lower branches to get longer. This suggests to the viewer that there is a great deal of rocky outcropping and that other trees nearby affect the wind velocity.

It has been said that if you are able to communicate to an independent viewer

Fig. 6-3.

the exact landscape where a tree was growing, you have mastered the art of bonsai design. For this reason, rock plantings, *saikei*, and group plantings are shunned by purists who feel that the bonsai should stand alone and does not require the trappings of rocks to give the impression of a rocky environment. In a sense, I agree with this philosophy; however, the use of some natural-looking accompaniments makes an even greater design statement.

In higher altitudes and the desert, trees will often exhibit a summer dormancy. In extreme environments, the tree is simply unable to cope with the high temperature, the wind, lack of humidity, and lack of rainfall. Trees that grow in these areas simply protect themselves by becoming dormant. Succulents store their own water. Cacti not only store their own water, but they lose their leaves completely in order to prevent desiccation. Some junipers and pines exhibit this summer dormancy in extreme desert areas. They simply shut down. Growth stops. White root hairs cease to exist. They protect themselves by turning a dark brown color and cease to function entirely. When fall arrives bringing cooler weather and new rainfall, the tree then seemingly

Fig. 6-2.

comes alive and puts out a short period of growth. Trees in these areas sometimes exhibit two annual rings every year—a large annual ring is produced in the spring and a smaller annual ring is produced in the fall. By totally removing new growth in the spring, secondary growth proportionate to the scale of the branches is produced and contributes to the effect seen in trees that are struggling to survive. See **figs. 6-2**, **6-3**, and **6-4**.

Fig. 6-5.

Fig. 6-4.

Direction of Wind

In **fig. 6-5**, the direction of the wind is coming from left to right in this coastal setting. From the amount of foliage on the tree it's clear the trees are really quite pampered by the amount of moisture in this humid area. Vegetation is lush and the trees are tall and almost vertical, like the formal upright, except that the branches on the right side are considerably longer than the branches on the left. In addition, you can see the effect of turbulence. The vegetation down below looks complete and symmetrical, and it is com-

pletely covering the ground. On the base of these trees, you can see the lower branches are considerably longer than the ones on the left, but at least there are branches on the left as well. This would indicate there is a lower wind speed toward the soil surface than there is up above. And finally, notice the tops of the trees. There is no vegetation at all toward the windy side, which indicates that not only is the wind strong but it is constant—and very damaging to the growth of new buds. Straight trunks indicate a strong prevailing wind, but not enough wind speed to actually cause the tree to grow in a crooked fashion. You can learn a lot from just looking at the style of a tree.

If this were a bonsai, you should be able to duplicate all these effects on your tree, and an independent viewer would come up and would be able to know that your tree was growing in a protected area at the coast. You should be able to communicate this to anyone who looks at your tree. It's a consistency of style, and it is the nicest way to design your trees.

Fig. 6-6 shows a similar situation,

Fig. 6-6.

except that the terrain has been changed. You can see by looking at the foliage on the surface of the soil that the ground speed of the wind is very minimal. The ground is completely covered with various grasses that are in bloom, as well as lower bushes and shrubs that are doing quite well. The growth is coming out in all directions, even toward the prevailing wind.

Nearing the climax trees above, which happen to be Sitka spruce, the effects of the terrain on these trees start to show. Notice the trees that are growing out on the edge of the cliff. They are completely unable to grow upright. The trees are bent away from the wind. The lower branches are quite evident, and as you go toward the top of the tree, the branches remain just as long.

Erosion causes other changes. A windswept tree at the beach may have a straight trunk. In more harsh environments, the trunks are crooked, going away from the wind, but once in a while the trunk leans toward the wind and the branches are swept in the opposite direction. This is because the trees grow in very soft soil and sand or in areas where water erosion is causing the trees to lean toward the source of the erosion. The source of the erosion of course is the wind and the rain coming from the coast. In times of storm or high tide, water will wash up and start to erode away and expose roots on the ocean side of the tree. The tree gradually starts to lean in, but tries to recover by growing stronger roots away from the rain, wind, and water, creat-

ing a stronger base. Eventually the tree stops leaning, but it is still in a bit of an unstable situation.

Previously, I mentioned the importance of having stable rootage on the sunny side, or the warm side, of the tree. The warm side of the tree is where the sunlight is and where the number one branch is not. In this case, nature is creating quite an unstable tree, because the roots are growing on the cold side of the tree, underneath very long and dense lower branches. The number one branch, number two branch, and so on are usually located on the down-wind side of the tree, and so are the roots. This increases the unstable situation, and the tree will continue to lean toward the wind. This creates some spectacular coastline scenes. These tree designs are used as logos for various coastal golf course resorts, hotels, and vacation areas.

Alpine

What **fig. 6-7** shows is an extremely stressed tree, but look at some of the individual features of this tree. It is a fir tree, which is obviously quite old, perhaps three to four hundred years old. Notice that it is straight, it is vertical, and this is a trunk line associated

Fig. 6-7.

with the formal upright tree—except notice the extreme difference in the windswept style of this upright tree. The lower branches are about the same length as the upper branches, which would indicate that the wind direction is constant and that the base of the tree is just as exposed to the wind as the upper portions of the tree.

In yet higher alpine areas, vegetation is not allowed to grow as high as this. Approaching extreme timberline, it is impossible for vegetation to exist at all. Any at all is only very low-growing shrubs, bushes, annuals, and perennials able to survive underneath the protection of the snow cover for most of the year.

Desert

In the desert there are completely different forces on trees. **Fig. 6-8** shows a fine old tree struggling to survive in an area with an altitude of about 2,000 feet (600 m), but the average rainfall in this area is only about four inches (10 cm). The tree is forced to have deep, penetrating roots into the sandy soil in order to survive. Obviously there is a high amount of ultraviolet light. The prevailing wind is constant, and there is a great deal of *jin*, *shari*, and

saba miki on this tree, which adds to its interesting form and texture. The branches able to survive are on the leeward side of the wind and they are sparse; they are very compact needles.

This is a tree that exhibits two annual rings per year, so it would be difficult to date, even with a core sample of its rings. Notice the number of unsuccessful tops. This tree has tried to form numerous different apexes over time, and the branches are also inconsistent in length and size. They vary in shape and in direction. This should indicate a different sort of wind pattern. This would indicate inconsistent wind that swirls. It would indicate that a number of rocky outcroppings are nearby. It would also indicate that the prevailing wind is not strong.

Coast

Here in **fig. 6-9** is a completely different style of windswept tree. It is quite obvious this is the coast, not because the coast is visible in the background, but because of the shape of the tree. Bonsai designed in this fashion should communicate that to the viewer without such trappings as gravel or sand around the base of the tree. Visible is

Fig. 6-8.

Fig. 6-9.

lush foliage against the cliff, which would indicate a somewhat strong wind. Lower branches going out towards the wind also draw in the viewer. These indicate a lower wind speed toward the ground, and that as we go up in this tree we can see the tilting of the apex, which would indicate that there is a much stronger wind up at that height.

The tree is fairly tall, indicating that the wind is not strong enough to prevent growth at that height, and also indicating that, in spite of this strong directional wind, it is also a wet wind. Notice the amount of foliage. Notice the number of successful branches on this tree.

Fig. 6-10 has a slightly different effect, with an exposed rocky outcropping near the ocean, and we have a pair of trees that demonstrate the effects of wind. Toward the bottom of these trees is lush foliage, with long branches going toward the leeward side. Going up the tree, the windswept effect is really quite directional, with branches only away from the wind. Notice particularly how the tree in front is able to protect the tree in back, and notice the slight gradation in the

amount and size of foliage. About two-thirds of the way up the tree, there is a group of heavy branches on the first tree. Notice the effect on the second tree. The presence of those branches make it possible for the second tree to have even more thick branches at an equivalent height on that tree as well. If there are three thick branches on the first tree, then there are probably 10 even thicker branches on the second tree, which is using the front branches in order to protect the growth for itself. The windswept style uses this natural clumping of branches. In designing bonsai, consider this as well.

With all the other styles, it is advantageous to have branches well distributed around the tree. Prune out congestion in order to allow sunlight to hit all the branches as they pinwheel around the tree. With the windswept style, an unusual exception comes up. To duplicate nature, it's possible to style by clustering branches in one area. In pruning a windswept style from nursery stock with three branches in close proximity, consider the windswept style. Retain all three branches and wire them together as a single branch. This will give a quite natural effect, what we see in coastline windswept styles.

Gorge

Fig. 6-11 shows the extreme effects of wind coming through a gorge. In the photo, we see only the right-hand half of a V-shaped gorge. There is a similar rocky outcropping toward the left, out of view of the picture. Wind is funneled through this gorge at such a high speed, it is impossible for vegetation to grow out from these rocks. These are Englemann spruces, which are struggling to survive in these rocky ledges and crevices. Any growth outside the protected area of vegetation is immediately desiccated by this tremendous wind. It's easy to look at this environment and imagine that an average

Fig. 6-10.

Fig. 6-11.

speed of the wind here would be in excess of 60 miles (100 km) an hour. Gusts of wind have been recorded in this area over 100 miles (160 km) an hour on a regular basis. In visiting this site, I have noticed that it is impossible to stand upright just to view this one area. Notice in particular the number of dead branches. As new growth comes out, it is a test by the plant to see if it can survive. If it doesn't, the little twig will remain as a dead testament to the tree's past attempts at clustering its foliage. All these unsuccessful attempts remain on the tree and add an incredible amount of twigginess that windswept bonsais can duplicate. To create a really nice, wonderful effect in pruning bonsais, then leave as much twigginess of branches as possible. Wire a live branch into place, a curved shape after stripping off the bark. The wire will move the green branch without breaking and the extreme twigginess of the branch will add to the windswept effect.

THE DRIFTWOOD STYLE

Jin, Shari *and* Saba Miki

Just as the name implies, the driftwood style indicates a great amount of deadwood on a bonsai. Obviously, if it is just a few little twigs, a dead top, or perhaps a hollowed-out trunk, the name driftwood could not be applied to this style. This style epitomizes the display of deadwood, and deadwood is best represented as beautiful, sweeping wood with much texture and character on its surfaces. At the beach, some of the pieces of driftwood lying in the sand are attractive. These same shapes can be copied in bonsai to give a very unusual effect. **Fig. 6-12** shows a driftwood-style bonsai. The sweeping curves of the driftwood are really quite obvious. There is a great amount of *jin*, *shari*, and *saba miki* on this tree and it is kept displayed for obvious reasons. It would be easy to have the foliage on this tree cover up this beautiful wood, but it would lose the wonderful effect. This is a driftwood style that is also windswept. It is obviously possible to make a driftwood-style tree that is not windswept. Driftwood styles can produce formal upright trees as well. As with all bonsai styles, there are considerable areas that are difficult to define. These are intermediary or transitional styles between two styles. It is quite conceivable to have a slanting-style tree that exhibits some driftwood, but not enough to call a driftwood style. It might be a slanting tree that is sort of slanting, but sort of curved as well, so

Fig. 6-12.

Fig. 6-13.

it is difficult to call it slanting or an informal upright tree.

Fig. 6-13 shows a tree that exhibits some *shari*. Along this trunk line, there is some deadwood. The deadwood is not completely obvious. It might be missed on a walk through the woods. In bonsai, however, the obligation to the tree is to keep it healthy and provide its care. This situation must be treated to make sure this wood prevails. Here is a dead area of a trunk partially covered by rotting bark. This bark must be peeled off or moisture will be trapped underneath the loose pieces and start the disease process. All plants have a tendency to return to compost when they are ignored, especially if they are subjected to excess moisture and fertilizer. For a bonsai, it's important to keep moisture off areas where it is not needed. Foliar fertilizer has a tendency to rot areas like this. Deadwood tends to turn dark and the beautiful driftwood will be lost. This area should be scraped clean and treated with lime sulfur or other preservative in order to maintain the health of this tree. At the higher altitude where this tree originated, there is enough ultraviolet light and lack of rainfall so that this *shari* does not need to be protected, but at lower altitudes these areas must be scraped clean or they will simply rot away and the style be ruined.

Tools

In my basic bonsai tool roll, I always keep a set of simple carving tools: a gouge, a chisel, and an angled carver. The angled carver is simply a chisel that makes a quick right-angle turn and is sharpened at the end of the right angle so I can carve things inside little hollows and crevices. Carving tools similar to this are available in any woodworking supply store. In addition, I like to keep a common pocket-knife that has three or four different sizes of blade. Many of my students keep a Swiss army knife nearby because of the number of tools included with the knife. Such interesting tools might be a leather punch, and even a corkscrew, which is useful for digging around in little crevices. Various sizes and shapes of blade available with these combination knives make them highly suitable as basic bonsai tools. In addition, I enjoy making *jin* and *shari* just with the use of simple pliers. Household pliers can grab a branch, twist it, and break it off just as if nature had torn it away. The resulting scar is really quite natural-looking as compared with a clean cut made with a pruning tool.

Larger pliers, such as a vise grip or a channel lock, are suitable for larger branches or trunks where you need to span a greater distance than the common household pliers can do. Bonsai tool makers manufacture a pair of pliers called the *jin*-making pliers. These are a combination pliers that have a chisel on one jaw, which is used for scraping away wood. The jaws themselves are highly serrated for the removal of bark. More advanced students can use power tools to do carving. Wood carving can be done by hand, but it is somewhat tedious, and greater results can be realized in a shorter period of time by the use of power tools.

One of the tools I recommend is the rotary motor tool. It is a tool that accepts small burrs with a one-eighth-inch diameter shaft. This tool rotates at high speeds and can be used for carving of small details. There are larger, similar-design tools that will accept a one-quarter-inch shaft, which are really much better. They are a more expensive tool (perhaps twice as expensive) but the variety of bits that can be inserted in them is much greater. Not only can you put in a one-eighth-inch shaft burr, but you can put in larger drills and carbide bits as well, for a larger variety of carving. A detail carver, which is an impact carver used for woodworking, is a tool I highly recommend. It is probably the tool which I use most often. It is a power tool that is safe to use, and only operates when the bit is actually placed against wood; otherwise, it just has a humming sound that tells you that the motor is on. It operates in a reciprocating manner, rather than rotating a burr. You attach interchangeable chisel-type bits to the end of this detail carver and proceed from bottom to top. You can add lots of nice little swirls and twists to bend your wood artificially and add interesting grain and texture that did not exist before.

Another tool that is quite popular among bonsai professionals and people who work on larger material is the die grinder. This is a tool I cannot recommend for a beginner or someone with weak hands, as it moves a lot of wood in a hurry, is very noisy, and takes a very steady hand to control. It is similar to operating a router freehand and requires a great deal of concentration and strength. The advantage is that a great deal of wood is moved in a hurry. The disadvantage is that you have to secure your work very carefully and

Fig. 6-14. A windswept-style San Jose juniper, juniperus chinensis 'San Jose'.

have the hand strength to control your bit; otherwise, it can launch itself out of control at a moment's notice. But this is a tool that is used very often.

For the extremely adventuresome, I will occasionally suggest a chain saw on a bonsai. I have equipped a chain saw particularly for bonsai purposes by inserting a handle into the small hole at the far end of the chain saw bar. This gives me considerable leverage with my left hand while I operate the trigger with my right hand. This keeps the saw from flashing up into my face as I'm trying to carve out an area using the end of the chain only. It is not for the timid and I would not recommend the use of the chain saw to people who are unfamiliar with this tool. But if you are comfortable with a chain saw in your hands and you use it on a routine basis, then get an 8″ (20 cm) handle and put it in the hole at the end of the bar to protect your whole hand. Obviously, the carving that you can do is rapid and not a great deal of detail is possible with a chain saw, but for larger bonsai that need large amounts of wood removed in a hurry, this is one way of accomplishing this task.

Carving Methods

In any art class or sculpture class, it is very difficult for the teacher to try to teach the student how to visualize a project. A few techniques work for me. One is to have a model to work from. For carving *jin*, *shari*, and *saba miki*, I often find that it is easier to have a wonderfully shaped piece of driftwood from the beach on my bonsai bench. I can look at the boring bonsai that I have in front of me and look back at the interestingly shaped piece of driftwood and get some ideas and inspiration on how to carve a straight, flat piece of wood. By placing the driftwood nearby, I can visualize the best way to carve an uninteresting piece of wood.

I can transfer some of the pattern by pencil or pen over to the bonsai and this will indicate to me where I would like various curved pieces of wood, or where I might position a knothole or hollow. I can also draw the type of grain that I would want to have around these knotholes in order to make my carving look interesting and natural. It is possible also to study other drawings of deadwood, other trees that contain deadwood, or even just boards or pieces of wood that you happen to have around. Keep these pieces around as study models to help you to carve your bonsai so it looks natural and interesting.

Always remember that you are carving after removing the bark. Before you begin your carving, make sure that you have totally defined the live area of your tree. Carve into the cambium area, which is the slippery part of the tree right below the bark, and make sure you define the *jin* area all around. Make sure that you consider the biology of the plant as you are carving dead areas. Make sure that you have supplied the plant with enough live cambium to provide nutrition to the live branches that you want to retain.

Timberline trees, such as this magnificent specimen near timberline, **fig. 6-15**, provide inspiration for *jin*,

Fig. 6-15.

shari, and *saba miki* carving. Notice the extent of the driftwood, notice the position of the driftwood, and notice the amount of texture you can put on a tree to make it look as though the tree is struggling to survive. I have found that if you have some deadwood on the tree, it is better to have deadwood in several places on the tree. Bonsai that have only a dead top are usually a little puzzling to look at. The viewer will wonder what sort of environmental conditions would kill only the top of the tree and none of the branches. Similarly, if only the end of one branch is dead, it makes the viewer wonder why. Try to explain why the tree is hollow. Do this by adding other driftwood elements to the tree to indicate that the area is now rotted away and has been hollowed out by squirrels. The presence of *jin*, *shari*, and *saba miki* together on a tree complement one another. Try to include several of these elements all at the same time for a wonderful effect.

Wood Preservation

As mentioned briefly above, it is important to make sure that the deadwood on the tree is preserved. It is a shame to go through a process of creating this wood only to find that in a brief period of time it is turning black and falling off. Normally, a few things are done to this wood. First it must be scraped clean completely. Notice that most of the deadwood preserved in nature has lost all its bark.

The cambium layer underneath the bark is the softest-growing area of the tree. The cambium's function is to create heartwood on the inside of the tree and to create a protective bark on the outside. Once the tree has died in an area, this soft area becomes very susceptible to infection by fungus and disease.

Observe that on this beautiful tree in **fig. 6-16** most of the bark has peeled off over time from freezing and thaw-

Fig. 6-16.

vide longer protection. This is true of *jin*, *shari*, and *saba miki* as well. Before applying a product such as lime sulfur, be sure the wood is completely dry and porous and partially bleached out by the sun.

Fig. 6-17 shows a collection of branches at a high altitude with lichens on them. The lichens are wonderful and I have tried to preserve them at lower altitudes, but I am always unsuccessful. After about a year of watering the plant, the lichens that have grown on the outside of the bark will turn dark and die because the natural conditions under which they grew are no longer present. It is similar to trying to take a small clump of moss from the mountains to grow in your garden. It doesn't thrive because the conditions are different. This is true with lichens as well. These are beautiful attachments to the trunks of old trees, but unfortunately on bonsai they have to grow naturally under the conditions in which the bonsai is growing, or they won't grow at all.

ing and has been bleached by the strong ultraviolet light in the area. Take your *jin* and *shari* and scrape off the bark immediately while it is still soft. Allow the bonsai to sit in the sun for a few months in the summer and wait until the sun naturally bleaches and dries out this former cambium layer. By allowing this layer to dry and bleach out, you have made the wood just a bit more porous. Once it is absorbent, then artificial preservatives can be added to the wood, such as lime sulfur. If a material such as lime sulfur or wood preservative is added while the wood is green, the preservative has a tendency to simply bead up on the wood. It will not penetrate and it will not protect as well as if you had waited until a little later.

Consider if you were to build a new deck outside your home, and you took the green wood and attempted to put a wood preservative on it immediately, it would bead up and not penetrate very far, and would stay wet and sticky too long. However, if you were to wait a few months until the wood was completely dry and porous, the wood preservative would attach itself to the wood, would penetrate more deeply, and would pro-

Fig. 6-17.

THE BROOM STYLE
Hoki Dachi

DESIGN CONSIDERATIONS

The broom style gets its name from a Japanese-style broom. The brooms we commonly see now don't have quite the same shape as a primitive type of broom formed by wrapping straw around the end of a stick. Some of the very early types of brooms found in Japan resemble the broom style when inverted. The stick, or the handle of the broom, if set down, puts the tiny pieces of straw in an upward position. It creates a somewhat inverted triangle that resembles a tree. The broom-style tree doesn't really look exactly like this, but it evokes a certain image and the name has stuck.

Evergreen Versus Deciduous

The broom style favors deciduous trees for several reasons. Probably the foremost reason is just the shape of most deciduous trees. Deciduous trees have more or less an upright growth habit and the ability to sprout and resprout, creating a very intricate pattern as the tree reaches toward the sky. Even very young trees immediately start demonstrating this pattern. Go to a nursery and purchase a small street tree, and in the crown of the tree the beginnings of what might look like a primitive Japanese broom are visible. When a deciduous tree loses its leaves in winter, there is no foliage to catch large amounts of ice or snow. As a deciduous tree ages, it has less of a tendency to have horizontal branches than does its counterpart, the evergreen tree. Even in older trees, this basic upright twiggy

Fig. 7-1. A good study model for the broom-style bonsai is an isolated pasture tree such as this oak.

form is prevalent. The secondary and tertiary branches in older deciduous trees are quite striking, both in summer with their leaves, and in winter with all their secondary ramifications. This is attractive in a good broom style. Try to achieve this degree of detail.

In addition, because deciduous trees lose their leaves every winter, they start out fresh in summer with no foliage at all. The insides of the trunk are warmed by the sun and additional sprouts are able to start anew inside all these branches without interference from foliage. Contrast this with evergreen trees, which in the spring are already covered with foliage. Back budding is therefore impossible because of the lack of light inside. Over time, the deciduous tree has developed an increased ability to back bud that is just not found on conifers. In the deciduous varieties available, most are able to survive complete defoliation in midsummer in order to promote back budding and decrease the size of the leaves as they come out with secondary growth. Use this artificial defoliation in midsummer as a way of decreasing the size of leaves and increasing the degree of scale and the illusion of age. If two bonsai are the same size, the one with smaller leaves will always look as if it has a larger trunk simply by comparison. The tree with the larger leaves will look younger, and the trunk will look smaller.

It must be noted that there are extremely old, fine bonsai that are deciduous and yet are trained in the classic pine tree shape with horizontal branches layered into clouds of foliage. This is quite an artificial style, not normally seen in nature, but it is beautiful enough anyway. Sometimes, in older deciduous trees, the branches tend to be brought down horizontally, simply because they have gotten longer and are starting to sag from their great weight. Almost every community has a fine old tree that was planted hundreds of years ago. By studying these trees, it is clear that the angle of the branches coming out from the trunk is considerably lower than it would be for younger trees of exactly the same species. So it is true that, over time, even deciduous trees will slowly sag to an almost horizontal pattern of branching. In bonsai, exaggerate this and artificially age trees by moving upright branches into a more horizontal position. The pine tree shape of strict horizontal branches is simply an exaggeration of this tendency. Some growers choose to use the horizontal method because it promotes back budding. In the broom style, all the actively growing buds are on the outside perimeter of the tree or in the top crown. By using the design of strict horizontal branches and clouds of foliage, sunlight enters the inside of the tree and creates more buds closer in towards the trunk. What results is a faster-growing tree that is easier to maintain. It is simply a matter of style and choice, because both are seen in nature and in bonsai style.

The broom-style design does not favor the evergreen tree. Evergreen trees naturally have a more horizontal branch even in young trees, but partic-

Fig. 7-2. **Wisteria chinensis** *grows naturally as a weeping broom-style bonsai.*

ularly as the trees get older they have a tendency to sag from their own weight, as well as from the weight of snow, frost, and ice. To imitate nature, notice that not only are older evergreen branches horizontal, often they are below horizontal. This is most easily seen in the higher-altitude regions, and can be seen among older evergreens in cities and towns. Over time, evergreens, and particularly conifers, have lost some of their ability to back bud on old wood because there has been no necessity to do so.

Described below is the pruning cut for establishing the beginnings of a formal *hoki dachi*. It is a sharp V-shape cut in a trunk, just a few inches (cm) above the root buttress. This cut on a pine tree would surely kill it. Some conifers might survive, but they would survive poorly. This same cut on a maple or an elm creates the desired broom style. Very few conifers will survive this treatment. Some exceptions are the sequoia, redwood, dawn redwood, swamp cypress, and certain broadleaf evergreens when they are pruned in late spring. Think of a boxwood hedge. Pry apart the branches and look inside. Notice that the inside of the hedge is completely bare. Evergreens have a tendency to do this and it looks a little odd on bonsai to have growth only in the outermost tips. Once the inside dies away, on most evergreens it is very difficult to get this growth back. Therefore, the broom style is usually reserved for deciduous trees.

69

VARIATIONS ON
HOKI DACHI

By Species

To understand what the broom style appears like in nature, consider some of the species that produce the broom style naturally. Consider a maple tree. A trunk comes up from the root buttress and almost immediately starts striking out branches at about 30 degrees off vertical. Numerous branches usually come up that start to form a twiggy pattern. These primary branches then divide into secondary branches, which then of course redivide into tertiary branches, pretty soon producing a large, spreading tree about as wide as it is tall, with numerous branchlets and sub-branchlets displaying a tremendous amount of twigginess. Consider the elm tree, with a slightly different pattern of twigginess, but lots of secondary ramifications too. A number of trees create a much taller, spreading canopy. These are usually the trees with compound leaves, such as the walnut. These are beautiful trees with a fairly open form. The spreading canopy is simply a series of multiple trunks that combine to make one tree.

The boxwood, by contrast, forms a natural broom style, but of course the outside canopy is the only area that supports any green foliage at all. Left untrimmed, the boxwood forms a more or less round-shaped tree, just about as wide as it is tall, and maintains this shape throughout its life. Several pines tend to form a broom-style shape rather than the single trunk shape. Three examples are the mugho pine, the tanyosho pine, and the Swiss stone pine.

Conifers that grow in slightly warmer climates don't have the snow stress high-altitude conifers are subject to and have a tendency to grow multiple branches and multiple trunks. The branches have a tendency to branch and rebranch, forming a natural broom style. The mugho pine is a high-altitude pine, but the multiple trunks are potential apexes. The mugho pine uses its ability to back bud to survive in the extreme cold in the Swiss Alps.

Sometimes the best bonsai for pines of this growth habit is simply to enjoy them as a broom-style tree. Heather is an extremely good example of a plant used for bonsai that is almost exclusively appreciated for its broom-style twigginess. The azalea is similar. It grows a bit wider than it does tall and has a tendency to throw out multiple branches that then turn into sub-branches. This extreme twigginess is easy to enjoy, just in its natural style. However, there is nothing quite as beautiful as a pine tree–shaped azalea. In Japan, these azaleas, which are often satsuki azaleas, are highly prized for their horizontal pine-tree shapes. The azalea is quite pliable when young and easily trained into almost any style imaginable. Left to itself, it will form a natural broom style. Trained as bonsai, it is most often trained into the classic pine-tree shape of horizontal branches and a single apex with a foliage triangle. Consider the shape of the poplar, or the Italian cypress. The first is a deciduous tree, the second a conifer, yet they both have similar shapes. They grow highly upright as compared to their widths and are prized for their multiple trunks and multiple branches, and as bonsai material they are best enjoyed in their natural shape.

Natural Shape for Species

All species have a natural shape in which they grow. Nurserymen and foresters can often identify a tree from quite a distance away without the use of the hand lens or, in fact, without seeing the foliage at all. A forester can look at the outline shape of a spruce on a distant mountain ridge and can tell that it is a spruce because of its characteristic outline. The branches on a spruce come out in a particular pat-

Fig. 7-3.

Fig. 7-4.

tern. The apex looks typical for this species, and the general height-to-width ratio for the outline shape will be a clue to identifying this tree from quite a distance. All species have their own characteristic outline shape. Know these shapes and try to make bonsai from their plant material. If you are trying to style a strongly upright tree into a cascading style, it is better to know beforehand that it is a strongly upright species. On the other hand, if you are trying to form a cascading plant and discover that the natural shape of this plant tends to be cascading anyway, you'll prune this plant differently to take advantage of the natural ability of the plant to form

the cascade.

The outline shapes of trees change with age. Lower branches, as they become heavier, take on more horizontal positions, even on deciduous trees. The large, spreading canopy of an old oak is different from the fairly tall, twiggy canopy of a fairly young oak tree. As a tree ages, the more horizontal nature of the branches has a tendency to allow more open spaces that can be seen through. On an immature tree it is very difficult to see the trunk, because, deciduous or evergreen, the outside tips of the branches, the leaves, and the foliage have a tendency to hide the trunk. The outline shape shows, but not the branch structure, certainly not the trunk itself. As the tree gets older, the branches start opening up spaces through which to peek into the tree, showing some of the horizontal branch structure as well as open sky in between branches. The only part that remains obscured is the top third of the tree. For this reason, in designing bonsai, intentionally trim away branches to leave these open spaces and achieve the illusion of age.

MULTIPLE TRUNKS

With a broom-style tree, it is sometimes difficult to deal with the problem

Fig. 7-5.

Fig. 7-6.

Fig. 7-7.

of multiple trunks. With a very young tree that has produced a wishbone or a fork in its style, these two main branches will start to divide and re-divide, but you'll have two competing tops. One top, obviously, is going to grow a little bit bigger and it's going to grow a little bit faster than the other. Normally it is the top that is growing toward the south. The weaker top is going to be cooled by the strength of the stronger top and will start to lag in growth. Most broom styles in mature trees are not perfectly round. The strong top will have its own apex. The weak top will have a separate apex far-ther down inside the tree. To achieve a balance in designing the trees, accom-modate the separate types of growth of these two trunks. The taller apex will have more secondary branches below it. The smaller apex will be almost an afterthought on the tree. The outline shape of a two-trunk tree will be a little bit asymmetrical and sometimes this can be really quite pleasing.

Fig. 7-7 shows a fine old pine tree growing in a desert. It has formed two obvious trunks. There are third, fourth, and fifth trunks here as well, but they are less obvious, less impor-tant, and less visible. Of primary con-cern is what to do with these two domi-nant trunks. The trunk on the left is obviously winning the battle, and is pointed toward the sun, toward the south. At the north end of this tree the slightly smaller trunk is starting to fail. The wilt in the trunk is due to lack of strength and presence of snow load, which on this tree has taken the top trunk and moved it down, so it func-tions more as a branch than a second-ary apex. This style works well for con-ifers trained up into the broom style. Isolate certain branches, so there are spaces in between them, allowing light inside the plant. Retain the general outline shape for the species, but exag-gerate the contribution of each individ-ual trunk. Isolate two trunks slightly from each other. Don't try to hide one trunk behind another. Allow each trunk to be viewed and let additional light inside the tree to keep it healthy.

GROVES

A grove is a combination of trunks and branches and outline shapes that com-bine to make a larger outline shape for the entire grove. Imagine five oak trees clustered together in the middle of a meadow. Perhaps a herd of cows or flock of sheep have pruned away the bottom branches of these trees. Imagine not only the outline shape above, but a nice trim outline below. When this grove is viewed in winter without its leaves, it's possible to study the branch structure. This branch structure crosses and recrosses itself over and over again and creates a general sort of twigginess, but it's clear which are the primary trunks, which are the secondary trunks, and how each contributes to the general outline shape of the grove as a whole.

In a forest planting for bonsai, by contrast, the design is different. In a bonsai forest, each tree has its own outline shape and there is rarely an outline shape for the forest itself. In a windswept grove at the beach, the trees combine to make one outline shape. In the oak grove in the middle of the meadow, the entire grove forms an outline shape characteristic of oak groves. Trees that grow close to each other will become almost as one tree. In the forest is a combination of grove trees as well as isolated trees that form their own distinct outline shape. In a forest planting, such issues as depth and variety are important. Often a forest will have trees of varying ages. The parent tree drops a cone that sprouts. At the base of the larger tree will be growing a smaller tree. The smaller tree, in its effort to grow out toward the light, will try to form its own individual outline shape. With a grove, it's almost as if all of the trees are roughly the same age.

SAIKEI

Just as in the forest above, the shapes of trees are affected by their surroundings. In a *saikei*, scale and the impact of the various elements used to create the landscape are the main concerns. Trees are only one element. Just as important are rocks and shrubs and ground cover and perhaps gravel or sand. A complete balance of these elements results in a miniature living landscape called *saikei*. All elements have an important and equal visual contribution. The outline shapes of trees as they come in contact with each other are similar to what we see in groves.

THE NATURAL STYLE

In my bonsai collection, I have some natural-style bonsai. I have some formal *hoki dachi*, and I have some trees that are intermediate styles, in between these two extremes. Neither is more correct than the other. They just represent different philosophies and different methods of pruning trees. When people come to visit my collection, I find it interesting that some of them think the natural style is far more beautiful than the formal style. Others are attracted by the beauty of the formal *hoki dachi*. You have to develop your own personal style in dealing with the broom style, but I will describe these two different extremes in style, so that you can learn where your taste runs.

It is difficult to describe any particular structure about the natural style, other than to say that most of the branches grow completely randomly. If you have enough random branches in a tree, eventually you sort of enjoy and appreciate the tree just for what it does on its own, without any trimming. Obviously all bonsai need trimming back; otherwise they will outgrow their containers. In my natural-style *hoki dachi*, I try to maintain the unpredictability of the angle of the branches. I try to make sure that crossing branches are not trimmed away. I try to make sure that the outline shape is ragged and not trimmed into the shape of a flame or a ball.

Fig. 7-8 shows an oak tree that has been maintained in the natural-style *hoki dachi*. Notice the aspects of the tree that are different from the formal *hoki dachi* in **fig. 7-3**. The trunk is a bit more irregular. The blemishes have

Fig. 7-8.

been allowed to show. Roots are longer on one side than the other, and smaller branches originate farther down on the trunk. There is the main leader coming up through the canopy or crown and, completely at random, large and small branches alike sprout from this central leader. On the right-hand side are large gaps with no branches at all. I've made no effort to fill these in, as it seemed counterproductive to forming the natural style for this species. Every possible angle of branch comes out from the trunk. Some are quite horizontal, some vertical, some branched, some unbranched. The general outline shape is rather rounded at the top but fairly square on the sides. The right-hand side sticks out a bit farther than it would in a formal *hoki dachi*. I have intentionally left the crossing and untrimmed branches, left some a little bit more twiggy than I would in a more formal tree. If two branches came out from the trunk at the same level, I left both. The sense of proportion is considerably different from that of **fig. 7-3**. Both these trees are exactly the same species and variety; still, look at the two contrasting styles.

THE SPROUT STYLE

The sprout style is quite interesting. When I was first experimenting with bonsai, some of the plant material I had access to came from under fence lines close to home. These were old hawthorn trees that had been trimmed by the maintenance staff of my school so many times that they no longer resembled a straight upright tree, but had a short squatty trunk with lots of multiple trunks. This was my introduction to the sprout style.

Since then, I have run across other similar situations. I was able to find a number of pine trees that had been similarly mowed next to an airport where the runways were being kept clear. These pine trees had been trimmed for a number of years to the height of about 8 inches (20 cm) and made wonderful bonsai subjects, provided you could get them out of the ground and make them survive. I have since experimented with hedge material. Quince naturally grows as a sprout style. Anyone who has ever grown quince knows the number of sprouts that come up from the base of the trunk. In addition, in my various ventures out to local nurseries, I have found plant material that has died back because of abuse or freezing weather. From the root has come a number of young sprouts that indicate that at least the plant is alive. Often these plants are back in the nursery boneyard where they are about to be discarded and can be picked up at little or no cost. Sometimes these trees make magnificent bonsai because these sprouts can be trained into individual trunks, and look quite nice in time.

The nicest bonsai that I have seen in this style came from material that naturally produces sprouts. Quince adapts really well to the sprout style, and a sprout-style quince bonsai is more appropriate than a sprout-style pine bonsai. Other plants that do well are listed below in the section on recommended species. Visit an ancient orchard, and you'll notice that many of the trees have reverted to a sprout style. Oftentimes the graft up above that was intended to produce superior fruit turned out to be not so superior when the orchard was left to neglect. When nature took over, the wild rootstock down below turned out to be the hardiest part of the fruit tree. What remains after about a hundred years of neglect is rootstock that has sprouted up and is really doing quite well. It is resistant to disease, and is growing quite vigorously. Often the fruit is insignificant, small and unshapely, but the flowers are quite beautiful.

Fig. 7-9 shows a very good example of sprout-style maple. This is a vine maple, *acer circinatum*, which was collected from the woods near my home. It is an extremely old tree, at least several centuries old. This type of tree is difficult to date because of the nature of the sprout style. There is a central trunk with several leaders that have tried to be successful in the confines of the rock in which the trunk was growing. Actually, the tree lifted out of the rock quite easily because the rock formed a natural container, or pot, and the roots were really very happy to be planted in my garden for a year.

Fig. 7-9.

MAKING A FORMAL
HOKI DACHI

The general idea behind the formal *hoki dachi* is to form a pleasing symmetrical broom-style tree from fairly old stock. Choose a fast-growing species, such as elm or maple. Make a V-cut right into the top of a four-inch (10 cm) -diameter trunk. The total height of the tree after cutting is about eight inches (20 cm). The rest of the tree is discarded, even if the tree was formerly 18 feet (540 cm) high. Because it's a fast-growing species, the tree will put out hundreds of new sprouts. Only two selected sprouts are saved, one at the top of each side of the V. All other sprouts are removed. These two sprouts are allowed to extend for one year. These same two sprouts then go through the same process. The two sprouts then turn into four sprouts. The four sprouts are cut, and eight new outer sprouts are saved. Each time the cut is made, the tree gets about one inch (2.5 cm) taller than it was before. Every year the number of branches on the tree doubles, but in a very formal and symmetrical pattern. In just a few years, there are 64 branches, 128 branches, 256 branches, and so forth. In winter these trees look spectacular.

Growth Principles

Obviously, as the formal *hoki dachi* is created, it looks quite odd at first to see a four-inch (10 cm) -wide trunk immediately taper into two very tiny little sprouts. In order to correct this, allow these two sprouts to grow for a complete year, unpruned and unchecked in any way. The plant is heavily watered and fertilized. These two small sprouts will reach up toward the sky in quite an enthusiastic manner because the roots on this tree have been left untouched. They may reach six or eight feet (180 or 240 cm) in length by the end of the year. In February of the following year, reduce these two branches to only one inch (2.5 cm) in length. At the tip of these two smaller branches, keep four new sprouts. These four sprouts should come up in random directions. You don't want to create a tree that looks like a fan. These four sprouts are allowed to grow for one complete year, unchecked and untrimmed in any way. The following February, these four sprouts are cut to one inch (2.5 cm) in length. In two years, a nine-inch (23 cm) -tall bonsai results, in three years a ten-inch (25.5 cm) -tall bonsai, and so forth. Each year the number of branches doubles. In a formal *hoki dachi* that has been trimmed for 30 years, the number of branches on the tree will have doubled 29 times. Put that figure in a calculator and figure out how many branches are on the tree at this time. It's huge. But you also have a tree which is only 38 inches (96 cm) high; the original eight inches (20 cm) of your trunk, plus 30 trimmings. In time, the original two sprouts don't look like sprouts at all anymore, but they look like considerably large branches. The trunk will still be the largest part of the tree, but because of this unlimited growth, you've developed very thick branches now where there used to be just two spindly sprouts. Your original V-cut will completely disappear. It will be overwhelmed by the diameter of these two branches and no scars will show at all on your tree from top to bottom.

PRUNING AND WIRING TIPS

For complete details on pruning and wiring bonsai, refer to chapters 11 and 12. The discussion here refers to individual problems pruning and wiring the broom-style tree only.

Bonsai branches are normally trained with copper wire. The problem with training broom-style trees is their extreme twigginess deep within the tree, making it difficult to get wire around the branches. For isolated branches, or to train the pine-tree style on deciduous trees, wiring is easier. I prefer to use the pinch-and-grow technique developed by the southern Chinese school of literati. In this school, students learn to shape bonsai by pinching the new buds as they arrive. Once a bud has been pinched, new growth appears. Among this new growth, you can pick and choose the buds you want and remove the others with tweezers before they become large. Once growth is extended in the proper direction for a period of time, pinch the bud again to prevent extreme elongation of the branch. Every time the branch is pinched back, new buds form all over it. Pluck out the unwanted buds with a pair of tweezers and allow the desired ones to grow. Using this technique, all styles and shapes of bonsai can be formed. It is a slow and tedious process, but it is done without any pruning tools other than tweezers, and it is also done without scarring. The elm in **fig. 7-10** is pruned primarily by this method. When I first acquired the plant, it was badly misshapen and had grown too tall. It had to be severely pruned back with pruning shears. I soon discovered that this particular kind of elm develops a greatly distorted trunk as the plant tries to heal itself. Since then, I have been able to shape and reshape these scars so that most are invisible now, and I'm starting to get a nice, twiggy branch structure. For the most part, the tree is left in its natural form and longer branches are allowed to

Fig. 7-10.

grow more vigorously than smaller ones. This is a rather modified version of the natural style; there are very few crossing branches but it is still natural, because it does not have the formality of the two branches turning into four, turning into eight, and so forth. It is a nice, pleasant compromise between the formal *hoki dachi* and the natural *hoki dachi*.

RECOMMENDED SPECIES

Fig. 7-11 shows a type of ornamental grass. In the broom style, ornamental grasses are used as accompaniment plantings. We see blood grass, iris, daffodil, even herbs such as rosemary and thyme are allowed to grow up as clumps and conform to the broom style. In this list of recommended species, first mention goes to general kinds of plants which can be classified as accompaniment plantings, or ornamental plantings, next to large bonsai. Some recommended species are: abelia, acacia, aralia, arbutus, arctostaphylus, azalea, berberis, buxus, cactus, camellia, carmona, ceanothus, celtis, cercis, chaenomeles, chaemacyparis, citrus, coffea, cornus, corokia, cotoneaster, cuppressus, currant, daphne, erica, euonymus, ficus, fuchsia, kalmia, macadamia, nandina, olea, parrotia, photinia, pieris, pistachia, polyscias, quercus, rhododendron, rosa, shefflera, serrisa, syrax, syringa, tamarix, taxodium, taxus, thuja, tilia, ulmus, vaccinium, viburnum, weigela, wisteria, wrightsia, zelkova, ziziphus.

Fig. 7-11.

THE GROUP PLANTING
Yose Uye

DESIGN CONSIDERATIONS

The Chinese arts of *p'en j'ing* and *p'en tsai* and the Japanese arts of bonsai and *saikei* are replete with tradition. When it comes to the group planting, certain traditional rules help the beginner get started. Sometimes traditional rules do not apply to untraditional types of planting, but everyone needs a starting place to learn some of the principles of putting together a successful planting. This chapter discusses traditional rules.

There are many differences between a grove and a forest which should be discussed here. **Fig. 8-1** and **fig. 8-2**, respectively, show the grove planting and the forest planting. Consider some of the observations possible about these two types of planting. In general, the grove is contained by a certain boundary. This boundary is, in the human sense, just a few yards, or perhaps as much as a hundred feet, but the boundary ends where the grove ends. A forest has a completely different purpose. A tree is placed in the back because it is smaller. It is intended to appear as though the smaller tree were the same size as the front tree, only it's farther away. This increases the sense of depth and increases the sense of being inside a forest rather than merely gazing upon a smaller grove.

Simple groves can be made with two, three, five, and seven trees, whereas it is much more difficult to make forests out of those small numbers of trees. In a grove, most of the trees are found at the same level as the root buttress. In looking across the root surfaces of a grove, it's clear that most of the trees have originated from seed at about the same time and all the trees in a grove are approximately the same age. In a forest, on the other hand, is a great variation in height. There is a great difference in height due to the differences in ages of the trees. Some of the parent trees are still around while the children are growing up. This is usually not the case in a grove. In a grove, all the trees are basically siblings. An additional major difference in the grove as opposed to the forest is the concept of a group outline. In the grove, the trees are approximately the same age and are found clustered together. In a forest planting, the trees are individuals. The distant trees are smaller, but again, that's simply because they're farther away, not because they're young trees. In the front of the forest planting are small trees, and they represent young trees. These are the seedlings that come from the parent plants toward the front of the planting. Small trees in the back of a forest planting are small only because they're farther away. They are large trees at a distance. Under these conditions, it is difficult to create a complete forest outline. Both the grove planting and the forest planting are considered to be group plantings because they contain more than one tree. When planting several trees together, there is a customarily pleasing relationship between the trunks. Trunks that are placed close together will have a tendency to lean out toward the light. Trunks that are placed farther apart will tend to stand up much straighter. This phenomenon is visible in this dead grove, **fig. 8-3**. Although the trees have died because of the harsh growing conditions, the general design that nature intended is obvious. The trees were growing up and escaping each other for light. Eventually their resources ran out. This is a beautiful study in the outline shapes of several trees in a grove setting.

Fig. 8-1.

Fig. 8-2.

Fig. 8-3.

THE CONTAINER

The most customary container for group planting is the flat tray. This is an extremely shallow bonsai pot, sometimes known as a *saikei* tray. Often the edge of the container is only one or two inches (2.5–5 cm) high. These are large pots in general, starting at about a foot (30 cm) wide, and going up to perhaps four, five and even six feet (129, 150, and even 180 cm) in length. The larger pots tend to be extremely expensive because they are difficult to fire. They always have drain holes with the exception of a *sui ban*, or water container.

In the *sui ban*, there are no drain holes, but only a swirling bluish-greenish mix (of pigment or glaze that resembles the water). Inside a specialized pot such as the *sui ban*, a large rock is placed as an island. On top of the island are placed various grasses, trees and shrubs to form a miniature landscape on top of the rock. For display purposes, the container is filled with water, which then serves as a reflecting pool. It makes a wonderful presentation to come across a display where the *sui ban* is used. From a distance is the island with all of its plantings on top of it. As the planting is approached, its mirrored reflection down in the water becomes visible. It makes a wonderful sight.

Most flat *saikei* trays or forest planting trays have numerous drain holes in the bottom. A 12-inch (30 cm) -long container, one inch (2.5 cm) high, can easily house seven trees. A wonderful project for beginners is to make such a planting from two- and three-year-old nursery stock. In terms of color, just as in bonsai, the dark glazes, dull browns, and grays work best for evergreens and conifers. If a broadleaf evergreen has shiny leaves, flowers, or fruit of any kind, the forest planting container is usually a colored glazed pot such as a sea green, a cream, a cobalt blue, or a dull turquoise color. Brightly colored pots, such as yellow ochre or brick red, and pots with calligraphy are reserved for the Chinese styles of *p'en j'ing* and *p'en tsai*. Brightly colored plants placed on grotesquely shaped rocks seem to suit these containers well.

Some forest plantings, such as the one in fig. 8-2, are planted simply on a flat rock. It's fun to go down to a local quarry or landscape supply store and pick out flat rocks used for masonry or stepping-stones or find interestingly shaped stones in the woods or forests near home. Remember that often rocks are protected in the national forests or wilderness areas. Please check beforehand to see if it is permitted to take these stones. Often a permit is necessary.

Flat trays can be made out of wood quite easily with simple carpentry tools. I make many of mine from strips of cedar siding; these pots drain well and as the landscape planting improves, it can be promoted to a ceramic pot later. In the middle of some of these plantings, a large rock can appear as if

Fig. 8-4.

at the ocean, or in the middle of a stream, or in the middle of a lake. You can use a simple raked-sand or gravel motif to achieve the feeling of water; try to achieve some of the natural effects seen in nature, such as this rock in **fig. 8-4**.

CREATING A YOSE UYE

Two Trees—So Ju

Perhaps the best way to think of two trees is the way the Japanese think of two trees, in terms of a family. It helps get a perspective on the two trees and how they should be presented in a single container. One tree should be noticeably taller than the other. The taller tree should have the thicker trunk. The taller tree should have the taller number one branch and should contain the greater amount of foliage. It is usually planted in the container with the root buttress predominating over the root buttress of the number two tree. In forest plantings, trees are normally numbered according to height. The number one tree in this case is the taller tree and the number two tree would be the shorter tree in the planting. I will use this designation to indicate the height of trees in the container.

The number one and number two trees in a *so ju* planting are normally planted as close together as their root buttresses will allow. Some family relationships can be described to help place these two trees about one-third of the way in from one side of the container. If the two trees are almost the same height, they could be considered as husband and wife trees. You can almost imagine the relationship between trees such as the mother and son or father and daughter.

Three Trees—Sambon Yose

The word yose means "grouping." If the container is divided into right half and left half, the best type of planting for a three-tree grouping is to clump the number one and number two trees together, as if to make a *so ju* planting. The smallest tree is then isolated and placed on the other side of the container. This seems to be the best combination of planting for three trees.

The way I usually arrange trees is to look at the number one tree carefully, and turn it around until the best presentation is toward me. This I'll consider to be the front of the tree. I do the same with the number two tree and the number three tree. Looking back at the number one tree, I'll look at some of its characteristics. If there is a bare spot on the right-hand side, this is an indication that the number two tree should be planted on the right-hand side in order to fill this bare spot. If the tree seems to be leaning strongly to the left, I would plant the number two tree on the right side, because, obviously, the number one tree would not be growing toward the number two tree. If there don't seem to be very many branches in the back of the number one tree, I'll try to position the number two tree slightly toward the rear, in order to fill in that space.

Five Trees—Gohon Yose

When positioning five trees in a container, it is best to position the number one and the number two trees together on either the left side or the right side of the container. The remaining three trees are usually not clustered together, but one of the three is placed toward the number one and the number two tree and the other two remaining trees are planted alone. The five-tree planting in **fig. 8-5** is a combination of three beech trees, *fagus sylvatica*. The tree on the extreme left has three trunks, making it appear as though the planting is actually five trees when there are only three. Notice the angle of the trees as they compete for light. These are intentionally planted so that they slant slightly away from each other, especially slanting

Fig. 8-5.

away from the number one tree. The smallest tree, the number five tree, is planted as far back in the pot as possible, in order to achieve the feeling of depth.

I found this five-tree grove of pine in a desert landscape, **fig. 8-6**. The pleasant leaning of all five trunks attracted my attention. I am standing at the south of this planting, looking north, and as you can see, the bark has been blistered and burned by the high degree of ultraviolet light in this desert landscape. This *yose uye* makes a wonderful study in nature on how to space trees so they are all clustered together and yet slightly uneven and unpredictable in their arrangement. A too-perfect planting sometimes looks artificial. A little bit of surprise and irregularity sometimes creates a more natural effect.

Fig. 8-6.

Seven Trees—Nahon Yose

Illustration **8-7** shows a natural arrangement of seven trees. These are pine trees next to a lake at a fairly high altitude, but the amount of rainfall they receive is modest. The trees seem to be all siblings and create a very pleasant grove. Notice that their trunk diameters are similar. Height is nearly identical, and it is quite possible that all seven of these trees started from a parent tree that died after producing these seven trees. Notice in particular the outline shape as these trees crowd together to protect each other from the summer sun. The trees on the left are obviously doing better because they are shaded by the trees on the right. I suspect that in a few hundred years the trees on the left will be continuing to thrive and the trees on the right will have become *jin*.

Fig. 8-7.

The Forest Planting

Fig. 8-8 shows the same forest planting later in the year that was shown in fig. 8-2. The miniature azaleas are in full bloom and the new growth has hidden the trunks completely. This forest planting is ready to be pruned, because I feel it's important to see the trunks of the trees in a forest planting in order to get the feeling of depth. The tallest trees have the highest root but-

Fig. 8-8.

tress. The shortest trees are buried quite low in the rear. The whole planting has been placed on top of a flat rock from the woods and it makes quite a pleasing landscape.

The Hundred Tree Style

As the previous photo shows, it is possible to have many trees in one container. It is possible to put 100 trees in one container, and I have done this on more than one occasion. But it is not necessary to have 100 trees to do the hundred-tree style. The hundred-tree style is characterized by the fact that it is not particularly worthwhile to count the trees. In the above example, there were perhaps 40–50 trees, but it started not to matter whether it was an odd or even number or in fact how many trees were in the planting at all—50, 60, 80, or even 200 trees. The overall feeling is one of great detail, great depth. It helps to have a very large container!

The Fallen Cone Style

Again, there are some gray areas between styles, and it is possible to mistake the fallen-cone style for the hundred-tree style as well as the sprout style, which has been mentioned earlier. The idea behind the fallen cone style is that a cone ripe with hundreds of seeds has fallen on the forest floor and most of the seeds in that cone have all decided to sprout at the same time. They compete for light, space, air, and

nutrition. But they're all exactly the same age. This is not a forest, it is an exaggerated clump of trees all competing with each other. Often these trunks are so close together, they actually fuse into one tree, and it's difficult to know whether they were started as many trees in one clump together, or whether it was an old stump which had numerous sprouts at its base. It's an interesting style and could be done with a variety of plants. I've seen this done with fruit trees, conifers, and even ornamental grasses. It's quite a stunning sight all of a sudden to see 40, 50, 60 trees all coming from one spot in a shallow pot. They have a tendency to radiate out away from each other as they seek light of their own.

Saikei

Saikei can be a group planting, forest planting, or sometimes even an individual tree. The thing that distinguishes *saikei* from bonsai is the emphasis on the landscape rather than emphasis on the tree itself. Some bonsai will have rocks in their containers. *Saikei* will have rocks in the container, but overall the general emphasis in *saikei* is to display the tree in its environment, as opposed to bonsai, where the rock is merely to suggest a possible environment for the tree. *Saikei* tend to be slightly larger than bonsai because of their containers, not the size of the plants themselves. It is difficult to

Fig. 8-9. A natural bridge saikei. There are 13 cypresses on this lava formation. The ground cover is linnaria.

plant a forest complete with rocks, understory plants, ground cover, and shrubbery in a container less than two feet (60 cm) long. By starting with quite immature material, sometimes less than a year old, plants can look really quite spectacular as rock plantings or as plantings on islands or all of the other landscapes that you can imagine.

Fig. 8-10 shows an example of *saikei* done with one tree. It is included here as an example of a group planting with one tree. The viewer doesn't fully realize that the vegetation on top of this coast planting is actually one tree. Several trunks come up from a broad base, giving the illusion of several trees

planted on top of this coastal rock. The planting could have been done with five, seven, or nine trees, but in this particular case, the same effect was accomplished with just one tree.

Fig. 8-10.

THE ROCK PLANTING

THE ROCK-GROWN STYLE—*ISHI ZUKE*

The rock-grown style is a general classification of bonsai and *saikei* that encompasses all the variety of plantings that can be put on top of rocks. In this type of planting, all the vegetation, foliage, and roots are planted up on top of a rock. In this case, the rock becomes the pot itself, although we see in some examples the rock may form an island or a mountaintop placed in a shallow viewing tray.

Island

In this type of rock-grown style, the rock itself is the island and on top of this rock is placed vegetation in an artistic and pleasing fashion. Consider **fig. 9-1**. Here is a large rock that is

Fig. 9-1.

located in a lake and, over time, vegetation has started to grow on it. There is a variety of ground cover, and there are some small shrubs and climax trees, such as the Douglas fir seen in the illustration. The effect is quite pleasing and relaxed, and gives a feeling of repose. There is a special type of pot called the *suiban* which has no drain holes. To use the *suiban*, place a large rock in the middle, plant trees on top of the rock, and, for display purposes, fill the *suiban* with water, to create a reflecting pool similar to what we see in this lake illustration.

Mountain

In the mountain rock-grown style, the top of the rock resembles a portion of a larger mountain. **Fig. 9-2** shows vegetation growing on top of a very tall rock structure that is part of a greater mountaintop. Trees growing in these conditions can grow in numerous styles. This illustration shows a fairly calm setting of the formal upright design primarily. If this were a mountaintop that had more wind, more of the driftwood or windswept styles would show. Imagine this large rock formation being placed in a flat, shallow *saikei* tray below, and you will have a mountaintop rock-grown-style bonsai.

Fig. 9-2.

Cliff

Vegetation often starts growing in the crevices on the sides of vertical cliffs. As trees grow out toward the light, they curve upwards and create a wonderful planting. In **fig. 9-3**, a natural example of a tree growing on the side of a cliff is displayed. The roots are encased inside the rock crevices of the cliff, and the tree curves upward toward the light.

Fig. 9-3.

Overlooking Water

The beautiful lakeside setting shown in **fig. 9-4** is only one of many styles next to water. This embattled tree is fighting to survive on this narrow ledge. It has few resources. There are only a few inches of rainfall per year and the high altitude and prevailing wind have formed a very nice *jin* on top of this tree. In Japanese gardens, we often see a tree that has been planted next to water. This could be a pine with a long low branch, or it could be a maple that leans in toward the reflecting pool. Duplicate this effect in a container by having water over to one side of the pot and a planting on the other side.

Fig. 9-4.

There is a container known as the Kawamoto pot, invented by Toshio Kawamoto. See the illustration. This container is divided into two sections. The outside edge is irregularly shaped and on one side is a drain hole. On the other side, it is a *suiban*, or water container. The two pots are divided by a ceramic dam built into the container. This allows a person to plant a tree, with or without a rock, on the side with the drain hole and lean the tree over the *suiban* section of the container. The *suiban* section for display purposes is then filled with water, and the tree is made into the overlooking water style.

Soil

If you used normal bonsai soil in rock plantings, you would soon discover that its highly textured nature and loose aggregate make it very difficult to use to secure a tree to a rock. For this reason, a special type of rock-planting bonsai soil known as muck is widely employed. There are many recipes for muck. I'm sure each bonsai artist has to develop a personal recipe for success. The muck I use is the discarded hemlock bark that I screen to make normal bonsai soil. The hemlock bark that I use is screened through common window screen, and the portion that remains on top of the window screen I use for the organic portion of my bonsai soil. The part that I would normally discard I sometimes save to make muck. It is a very fine powder of bark and in the presence of a small amount of steer manure, water, and a few tablespoons of cornstarch, it makes quite a thick, pasty soil that helps roots attach themselves to rocks. The mixture is too fine for use inside a container, but obviously there is a desiccation problem on the side of a rock.

This drying problem is fatal for plants in containers but we can take advantage of the increased dryness on the side of a rock to use this pasty bonsai muck. This specialized type of bonsai soil contains some nutrition from the added steer manure, and in time the roots will clasp the rock for increased strength. Care must be taken during the first year of watering so the muck is not excessively washed off the rock and the tree destabilized.

Clasping Techniques

There are a number of ingenious ways to attach a tree to a rock. Attach a split-shot fishing weight to the end of a small length of copper wire 22-gauge or smaller. The split shot is then forced into a rock crevice with a hammer and chisel until the lead adheres to the crevice by being spread out in all directions and being flattened and formed into the shape of the crevice. The wire is then attached to the rock by way of this lead fastening.

If you have a number of these devices attached to your rock before attempting the planting, you can arrange them so they will support the tree. Position the tree onto the rock and use these small lengths of copper wire around the root ball to fasten the tree to the rock. The lead and the copper are permanent, and they will be quite strong in holding the rock planting together. Cover the lead weights and the length of copper with muck. A slight variation in this technique is to use string instead of copper wire. You can still attach the split shot to the string, just as in the previous technique, except that instead of tying the tree root ball onto the rock with wire, you are making ties and knots with the string. The advantage of this technique over copper is that the string is not permanent and will not create possible problems for the root ball in the future. The string merely rots away. By that time, the roots have clasped the rock and do not need this additional support.

A technique that I use often is not very appealing aesthetically, but functions quite well. I attach the tree to the rock with muck, and then to support the tree while it grows, I simply wrap the entire rock with floral tape. The floral tape is green or black and is quite flexible. Over time, it will become brittle due to sunlight and will crack and fall off, but by that time the tree roots will have grabbed hold of the rock and will have created quite a stable rock planting. The tape of course can be removed as soon as the planting is stable. **Fig. 9-5** shows the types of soil and rocks plants have to endure in nature. **Fig. 9-6** shows a tree that is clasping

Fig. 9-6.

its rock quite tightly. There is a small crevice in this rock and it would be impossible to remove this tree. This type of stability can be achieved with bonsai rock plantings as well.

ROOT OVER ROCK—*SEKI JOJO*

Fig. 9-7 shows the tremendous root buttress of a tree that is attempting to grow on top of this rock next to the lake. The trees branch out in all directions over the top of this rock, and because they are growing on top of this rock in very few inches (cm) of top soil, the roots become highly exposed over time.

Fig. 9-5.

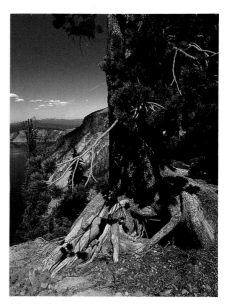

Fig. 9-7.

Habitat

The root over rock style is seen mainly in places with considerable erosion. Most trees do not like to have their roots exposed, but they will learn to survive over time if this erosion happens slowly. A tree starts to grow over the top of a rock. Erosion of topsoil due to water or wind or other factors gradually exposes the roots to the drying winds and ultraviolet light. The roots toughen, protecting themselves with a thick layer of bark similar to what is seen on the trunks of trees. The roots expand quickly to protect themselves from drying out. This style is seen next to streams and lakes, in thin topsoil on the edges of ravines or cliffs, and at the beach. The one thing these trees all have in common is that they have roots that are totally exposed going over the top or the sides of a rock. These make wonderful bonsai styles. It's possible to insert the rock underneath a root during transplanting, provided the root is of sufficient size.

Size of Root

For bonsai purposes, a root must have a diameter as large as a pencil before it can be exposed to the air without the benefit of soil. Smaller roots can be partially exposed on the soil surface, but without soil underneath the root, they have a tendency to dry out too rapidly. Larger roots can be totally exposed, either with air underneath them or rocks. If you try to expose your roots too fast, they will die.

Techniques

The simplest technique for making the root over rock style is to take a root ball and insert a pleasantly shaped rock into its center. With floral tape or string, attach many roots to the outside of this rock until they clasp the rock from all directions tightly. Then take the entire planting and plant the root ball and rock together in a tall pot.

Over time, you can either lower the rim of the pot if it is wood, or raise the root ball slowly, brushing away the soil from the roots with a small brush. This duplicates what happens in nature as soil becomes eroded away from the root ball. The roots will gradually toughen and increase in size, and over the period of a few years you can totally expose all of the roots and see the rock as well, and have created a very nice root over rock–style bonsai.

EXPOSED ROOT— *NE AGARI*

Fig. 9-8 shows a conifer growing on the edge of a rocky shelf overlooking a ravine. The rocky shelf provides stability for this tree although the rain and the wind in this area have gradually eroded most of the topsoil. This is an exposed-root style of tree, and bonsai planted in containers this high will form the exposed-root bonsai.

Fig. 9-8.

Habitat

Fig. 9-9 shows a very old tree growing in lava. Obviously, there will be no erosion in this area due to wind or rain or heavy water flow. Instead, what is shown is the inability of this tree to protect itself from the strong ultraviolet light in this area. The root buttress expanded over time and created an exposed root at the base of this tree as it grew.

By contrast, **fig. 9-10** shows a rock-

Fig. 9-9.

Fig. 9-10.

grown style at the coast. Different forces are at work on these trees. Obviously there is a great deal of rain and wind, and as the top soil erodes away, these trees are left with exposed roots. The trees are still stable and healthy because this erosion occurs over a long enough period of time so that the tree can recover from this adversity and strengthen itself for the exposure of its roots to the air.

Growing Techniques

Just as the root over rock style above was created, it's possible to create an exposed-root style by gradually exposing the roots over time. Plant the root ball in a tall container and gradually expose the root buttress. The following year, start exposing some of the roots that are larger than the diameter of a pencil. As the tree becomes older, the smaller roots down below will thicken and can be exposed as well. In a few years an exposed root–style bonsai will have been created.

Another method is to bare the root in winter. Use a large nursery plant that is growing in a three-to-five-gallon (13 l) container or larger. With the sharp pressure of a garden hose expose all the roots while they are still dormant. This technique must be completed no later than early spring. Observe all the exposed roots, trim away smaller roots in the top one-third of the root ball, and maintain the smaller roots in the bottom two-thirds. Then plant the tree in a bonsai container with these large roots exposed. When the tree comes out of dormancy, it is forced to grow bark on the exposed roots and draw moisture from the smaller roots that are contained in the bonsai pot with bonsai soil.

ROCK LANDSCAPING— *BONSEKI*

A related art form to the rock-grown bonsai style is *bonseki*. The only thing different from *saikei* is that the *bonseki* contains no plants. The rock planting is a tray landscape without vegetation. A shallow *saikei* tray is employed to contain a number of interestingly shaped rocks that suggest a certain identifiable landscape. These may be simple sand and stone gardens. With a few fist-sized rocks suggest a rocky outcropping at the beach, or with some lava cinders create a high-altitude volcanic landscape. The possibilities are endless for *bonseki*, but by definition, they contain no vegetation at all.

Saikei

Add ground cover or grasses or trees to *bonseki* to create a *saikei*. *Saikei* is a minature living bonsai landscape. With the art of *saikei*, it's possible to evoke all the landscapes that are seen in nature. In a *suiban*, create these two islands together, **fig. 9-11**, and cluster small dwarf trees on their crowns to duplicate this familiar natural setting at the coast.

In **fig. 9-12**, a similar scene has been created in a *saikei* tray with the use of three sandstone rocks and one juniper bush. The one tree is placed on top of the rocks that qualify it as a rock-grown style, but the juniper is trimmed to look like a grove of windswept trees at the coast. The predominance of the rocky part of this planting qualifies this as *saikei* rather than bonsai because of the stress on the landscape rather than the position of the bonsai on top of the rocks. **Fig. 9-13** shows how beautiful a *saikei* can be at any time of the year. This photograph was taken under moonlight in winter. It represents a small natural bridge that is found in the middle of a grove of conifers. The inspiration for these *saikei* came from nature. While hiking, I came across this one small tree trying to eke out its existence among these rocks (**fig. 9-14**). This type of inspiration can help you create *saikei*.

Fig. 9-12.

Fig. 9-13.

Fig. 9-14.

VIEWING STONES—
SUISEKI

For purposes of completing this chapter on rocks and stones that are related to bonsai, it's appropriate to discuss the related art of *suiseki*. Similar to *bonseki*, described above, it's possible to create landscapes with rocks alone. With *suiseki*, this is carried to the simplest extreme. *Suiseki* describe nature

Fig. 9-11.

by looking at a single stone. Suiseki are made of rocks that are quite interesting. Sometimes walking along the beach or in the mountains you may pick up a rock that resembles a face or an animal or a small house or some familiar object. You look at it, turn it over and over again, and admire it from different positions. This is what *suiseki* is. If you pick up an interestingly shaped rock that you wish to display, you can make a special wooden stand for it so it looks beautiful as an accompaniment to bonsai or standing alone by itself.

Examples of *suiseki* might include mountaintops, mountain ranges, even stones that look as if they have a waterfall coming down one side due to their crystalline structure. Sometimes they resemble thatched huts. Sometimes on the side of a stone is a beautiful impression of a flower, such as a chrysanthemum. Some stones are slightly hollowed so they will contain water, in order to evoke the feeling of a small lake. Some *suiseki* resemble human figures or animals or even mythical dragons. The finest *suiseki* are completely unaltered rocks. They are only polished with the hands as they are rubbed over time. Special stands are

made to display them in the proper orientation. This art form goes well with the other bonsai art forms. Displays that contain rock plantings, *saikei*, *bonseki*, *suiseki*, and other bonsai forms make the best displays.

Fig. 9-15. This large rock planting was created by fusing three maple trees together at the summit of the stone.

THE LITERATI STYLE
Bunjinji

HISTORICAL PERSPECTIVE

Around 1500 years ago in southern China, a school of thought, as well as a formal school of training, started developing called the literati style or the literati school. It was a center of philosophy, religion, and writing. Scholars, mathematicians, and astronomers would gather to exchange ideas and to look at each other's work. Poetry was studied. Artists developed their painting skill.

Along with these design ideas and philosophies developed a general sense of scholarship that encouraged professors to become skillful in many areas of knowledge. A similar notion developed during the European Renaissance; the Renaissance man was a scholar as well as an athlete. He learned the sciences, dabbled in architecture, philosophy, and religion, and tried to become as good in all subjects as was mentally and physically possible.

In the southern Chinese school of literati, this same notion was advanced. It was possible for a person to indulge in all forms of activity with like-minded individuals. The literati style therefore not only applies to the literati style of bonsai, but to the literati way of thinking. The literati bonsai style itself, known as *bunjinji* in Japan, has a unique artistic quality to it. It was thought that if you could master all styles of bonsai, you could graduate to a signature philosophical style that would transcend most of the other bonsai styles that were known at the time. The literati style, then, is not so much a style as a feeling or thought process. The notion was that a person who could master the arts, music, painting, landscaping, and poetry could utilize these resources to create a superior tree design. It would signify something loftier than one of the more structured styles available to bonsai artists at the time.

Fig. 10-1 shows a high-altitude tree that could represent the *bunjinji* style. It is an irregular style with two dead tops and a little bit of foliage, and it seems to rise from its base with a certain levity not seen commonly in a tree of this size.

In illustration **10-2**, similarly, in a coastal setting, is a tree that is mostly dead. Arranged here and there are a few sparse twigs and branches that are not particularly windswept, but it is an interesting design and a fairly large tree, and yet it has a certain lightness and ethereal quality to it.

Fig. 10-2.

Similarly, in **fig. 10-3** is a struggling young seedling in the mountain coming up out of a pile of rocks. Its various twists and undulations are not what you would normally see in classic bonsai design and yet the design works' well. It's easy to imagine this small pine in a round shallow dish and it would be pleasing to gaze upon.

In a rocky gorge, trees such as this unusual specimen in **fig. 10-4** are seen. This is a subalpine fir that does not conform to any particular style at all. The roots are clasping a rock and the

Fig. 10-1.

Fig. 10-3.

Fig. 10-4.

DESIGN
CONSIDERATIONS

Consistency

In all art forms, the concept of consistency is important. With bonsai comes a certain obligation to have internal consistency within the plant itself. This consistency must be suitable to the species. If we have a species whose branches are generally brought in a downward fashion, it would be better to continue that design. Illustration **10-5** shows a completely bare *jin* but it is a beautiful example of the literati style because it is consistent with itself, although it breaks many of the rules of classical bonsai design. It is not straight enough to be formal upright. It does not slant quite enough to be a true slanting style. One-third of the way down from the top is a classic barr branch that would normally be pruned away. And furthermore, the little hook-shaped piece at the top would be unpleasant in most bonsai design, and yet there is something very regal about this tree. It evokes an image of the location in which it is growing, and it communicates to the viewer the environment which shaped it. **Fig. 10-6** shows an unusually shaped tree as well. Certainly there is a windswept

tree is hanging out over a ravine. This slightly horizontal trunk has sprouted several new tops, and the effect is not only of a single tree but almost as if this single tree were forming a forest all by itself. This tree would be very difficult to pigeonhole in one of the classic bonsai styles. A portion of it is raft-style. A portion is a group planting. It is certainly an extreme slanting style. It could be root over rock, or it could be a rock-grown style. It could even be considered *saikei*. But I prefer to think of an unusual design like this as *bunjinji* because it has no particular style at all and yet it is beautiful.

Fig. 10-5.

Fig. 10-6.

quality about this tree, and yet the fork at the top represents a slingshot. The branches curve downward and then upward in a rather uncomfortable fashion. This is an interestingly shaped tree, and yet it is a beautiful tree to look upon as well. Some of these design features could be used in a *bunjinji* style.

Fig. 10-7. The extreme slant of this mountain hemlock, tsuga mertensiana, *is balanced by the heavy Japanese training pot.*

Fig. 10-8 is the same tree that was in fig. 10-1 except this time it has the other surrounding trees that have died. This creates a *bunjinji* type of group planting that would be spectacular in a *saikei* pot. Combine the effects of a miniature living landscape with *saikei* considerations, as well as the literati style of tree displayed in the landscape.

Fig. 10-8.

Fig. 10-9 shows a lone embattled pine hanging onto the edge of a cliff, looking out over a high-altitude lava lake. Obviously this tree is suffering greatly. It is probably close to 50 years old, and yet it has only a few little tufts of foliage on it. This tree is beautiful because it evokes the environment it grows in, and it causes us a bit of thoughtful self-reflection.

The Foliage Triangle

With the above examples of *bunjinji* are some of the shapes from classic bonsai design. There is a definite apex even though it is *jin*. You can see and identify some of the lower branches. Looking at these points, it's possible to imagine some semblance of a foliage

Fig. 10-9.

triangle. In designing a *bunjin* or literati style, keep in mind the foliage triangle. Even though plunging branches or other branches may sweep upward, or there may be highly curved branches and trunks, try to concentrate foliage around a foliage triangle and you will achieve unity of design.

THE CONTAINER

As with all bonsai containers, color is quite important when matching the container to the tree. The dark, unglazed colors of gray and brown and the tan shades are reserved for the conifers. The bright-colored glazes—the greens and blues, sea-green colors, turquoises, glazed black, and even the shinier shades of white, light blue, and cream—are reserved for those *bunjinji* plants that have a certain amount of color in their bark or stems, or fall-color berries, fruit, or flowers. The *bunjinji* container is most always round, hexagonal, or octagonal. The curves of the literati style are gentle and undulating, and the roundish curves of this type of container go best with this type of style. Often the outside edge is curved as well, with very little calligraphy or painted design. Usually the legs on the container number three and they are quite tall in relation to most bonsai containers.

The tree is positioned so the trunk is in the exact center of the *bunjinji* container. As the tree undulates upward, it is allowed to slant slightly off to one side. The root buttress is quite pronounced and visible. If the *bunjinji* container is two inches high, then the root buttress should be two inches (5 cm) above the top of the rim of the pot. By keeping the foliage sparse yet compact, it is possible to balance even the most extreme slanting-style *bunjinji* trees in these small round containers. One good indication of too much foliage is that the tree has a tendency to tip over. If a tree is situated correctly with a high, strong root buttress, if it undulates to and fro slightly from right to left, and if the size and number of branches on the tree are fairly sparse, it should give a feeling of visual stability as well as actual physical stability.

*Fig. 10-10. These natural curves make a nice **bunjin** style on this lodgepole pine, **pinus contorta**.*

94

PRUNING METHODS

BROADLEAF DECIDUOUS TREES

The broadleaf deciduous trees include about half the species that are used for bonsai. They have leaves that will fall off if the weather gets cold enough. Their outline shapes are rounded, not pointed like the conifers. At the base of each leaf is a bud where it is fastened to the branch. The direction of this leaf on the branch is very important. Consider its position carefully before pruning, because a new sprout will grow in the same direction.

Fig. 11-1. The maple family has opposite-facing buds and leaves.

The Elm Group

This group of broadleaf deciduous trees all have leaves that come from the stem in an alternate fashion. A leaf will appear along the branch to the right and the next leaf will come from the left side, and so forth. The trees that ex-

hibit this tendency are clustered in this group. To know whether or not your tree is a member of this group, simply trace the pattern of leaves along the branch. If you see two leaves coming out from opposite sides of the branch, it is a member of the maple group. If a branch or a leaf comes from the right-hand side and then alternates to the left-hand side farther down the branch, then it is a member of the elm group. At the base of each leaf stem is a bud that will become active when the branch is trimmed. This bud will also become active when the leaf stem is cut in half. It is also activated during any type of injury to the plant. The bud which is at the farthermost extension of the branch will be the most active. The buds that are closer in toward the trunk will be less active.

There are two types of tree within this group. Both types are alternate-branching types but the first type produces a regular array of right, left, right, left branching. The second type will produce a pattern that is right, left, up, down, right, left, up, down. The basic pruning principles for both of these types of plant are the same. At the base of the leaf stem is the latent

Fig. 11-2. The elm family has alternate facing buds and leaves.

bud that will appear after pruning. If you wish the direction of a branch to proceed over to the right, simply locate a leaf on the branch that is proceeding to the right and trim just beyond it. Cut halfway between the selected leaf and the next one out from the trunk. This will leave a small stub that can be trimmed off later. Pruning closer to the latent bud will often cause damage to the bud itself. Do not trim too close to this leaf or the new bud will dry out and growth will proceed in a completely different direction from the direction you had intended. If you want growth to appear on the underside of the branch, you need a species that has a regular pattern of right, left, up, and down. Focus on a leaf that is pointed downward. At the base of this leaf is the latent bud that you want to encourage. After you have identified this leaf, make sure there are two more leaves beyond. If there aren't, you must wait for them to grow. If they are already present, then you may cut or prune immediately. For those trees that have a regular array of right, left, right, left branching, and you want a new bud to go up or down, it would be necessary to wrap wire around the branch and twist it clockwise or counterclockwise so that new buds will be directed in an up, down, up, down fashion, rather than right, left, right, left. After this wiring, you may proceed just as above, identifying the direction of the latent bud and pruning just beyond it.

Fig. 11-3. Prune these strong maple shoots back before they harden off.

around the branch. It is extremely important for you to determine the direction of the branch that you desire. Then determine the pair of leaves you want to retain in order to promote the latent buds at their bases. With this group of trees, simply make sure that there are two pairs of leaves beyond where you prune before cutting halfway between the desired pair and the next pair. Whenever you prune a tree from this group, you should be looking at three pairs of leaves. The first pair is the desired pair that will produce growth in the proper direction. The next two pairs are simply extensions, where you are allowing growth hormones to get out into the end of the branch. Then when you trim halfway between the first and second pair, growth is con-

The Maple Group

This group of trees all have opposite leaves. Look at the branch carefully. If there are pairs of leaves coming out from the branch, then you have a tree that is a member of this group. Pairs of leaves will appear along the branch in various directions. Some trees have a tendency to produce opposite leaves in a regular array where the right and left pair are always horizontal. Other trees produce pairs of leaves that rotate

Fig. 11-4. Even some maples have flowers. Wait until after they bloom to prune.

centrated on the latent buds at the base of these two remaining leaf stems.

Compound Leaves

Although rare, a few broadleaf deciduous trees have compound leaves. These include the wisteria, pistachio, ash, and walnut. To determine whether or not a tree has compound leaves, simply look at the base of each leaf. If there is a small latent bud that is about to come out, then you know you have what is called a simple leaf rather than a compound leaf. In the compound leaf, one single leaf is made up of many leaves, usually in odd numbers, such as seven, nine, eleven, or even thirteen leaflets which make up one botanical leaf. The leaf stem is a single attachment to the branch and at the base of this leaf stem is the latent bud that you desire to grow for your pruning purposes. If you cut off a leaflet on a compound leaf, nothing will happen. This is another indication that you are dealing with a species that has compound leaves. In order to stimulate the correct kind of growth on trees from this group, you must remove the entire compound leaf in order to activate the latent bud below. Once you have identified your tree as a member of this group, simply trim the entire compound leaf as if it were a member of the elm group.

The Apple Group

There are a number of complex pruning problems in bonsai. A major difficulty is trying to maintain flowers and fruit on decorative trees, such as the apple, pear, peach, plum, and cherry, as well as some flowering types of tree, such as wisteria and flowering almond. For these trees, it is important to keep in mind that fruit appears on two-year-old growth and if you remove one year's worth of growth every year, your tree will never flower and therefore will not bear fruit. With this group, you

must identify branchlets as one year old or two years old. To retain flowers and fruit on plants simply trim away half of the one-year-old branchlets and allow the other half to become two-year-old branchlets. If you prune away half the tree severely every year and allow some of the other branches to age, these older branches will establish flowers and fruit and you can enjoy your bonsai. With this group of trees, if you are too judicious with your pruning and styling, it is possible that you will have a perfectly shaped tree, but you will have no flowers or fruit to enjoy.

BROADLEAF EVERGREEN TREES

These are a group of trees that retain their leaves in spite of the weather. When it gets cold, the plant simply goes slightly dormant, slows down its growth, and waits for the warmth of spring. Some of the more common trees in this group are the photinia, gardenia, azalea, rhododendron, camellia, boxwood, laurel, myrtle, and olive. Most broadleaf evergreens are shurbs rather than trees. This group of

Fig. 11-5. Broadleaf evergreens are pruned after they bloom.

plants is easiest to prune of all bonsai material. Simply wait for the bloom to appear, enjoy it, and as soon as it starts to fade, prune back heavily. By pruning back at this time, you are taking advantage of the new growth that will appear at the time the flowers begin to fade. At this point, the plants have the choice of producing a great deal of vegetation or putting energy into seed production. By trimming the branches back heavily just as the flowers fade, you are forcing the tree to put its energy into the production of new growth. Provided you take away no more than one to two years' worth of growth, these plants should bloom again the following year. In more severe cases where you are reducing a large nursery bush into a bonsai, you may have to prune away three, four, or five years' worth of growth. Under these severe circumstances, it is very possible that the plant will not bloom the following year, even though you are still trimming the plant at the proper time. Just as with the plant above, the direction of growth is determined by the direction of the leaf stem.

Fig. 11-6. This pine is not quite ready for candle pruning.

ble to observe the individual needles in the candle. This time is generally marked by a change of color from a brown or tan color to a green or chartreuse color.

Just as the individual needles start to emerge from this bud, gently rotate the entire candle until it separates from the branch. When this is done at the proper time, no small stem or core will remain on the branch. If this process is accomplished too late in the season, a pruning tool must be used rather than just the fingertips. In about four weeks, new candles will appear all over your tree; some where you want them, and some of course where you don't.

CONIFERS

The Pine Group

These trees grow with a spring growth of needles called a candle. The needles are bundled together in a cylindrical fashion and grow upward along a branch. There are two ways of pruning pine trees and the two methods are divided according to the health and degree of development of the pine bonsai.

First, consider the well-established, healthy, fully developed pine bonsai. For these trees, simply remove all the new pine candles as they start to open. The candle first appears as a small bud in late fall. It remains dormant through the winter and starts to swell as the pine sap rises. In early spring, the candle starts to swell and it's possi-

Fig. 11-7. These pine candles are perfect for twisting off. Notice the male cones below them.

With a pair of tweezers, simply select the candles that you do not want to allow to grow. Gently pull them off the branch or rub them out with the tip of your fingernail. Remaining now on the pine tree are myriad small candles that are growing in the proper dirction in your pine bonsai. These may be allowed to fully grow and develop for the year.

As the summer days lengthen to fall days, it is important to give this pine plenty of sunlight, particularly below each branch. Tear off all three-year-old needles and the bottom portion of all two-year-old needles on the pine tree. This will stimulate increased bud formation in the fall. These buds will produce the new candles for the following year and the annual cycle will repeat.

The second type of pine candle pruning is reserved for trees that have been recently transplanted, are not too well developed, or look a little bit weak or spindly. In late spring, the candles will be just opening up into the individual needle. The candle should be quite flexible, light green in color, and succulent. These candles should twist apart easily at this time. Remove three-quarters of the length of the longer candles. The tiniest candles should be left untouched. Medium-size candles are twisted in half.

The Juniper Group

The plants that are included within this category include of course the juniper, as well as arborvitae, cedar, false cypress, and true cypress. All these plants are categorized by having flat plates of growth that spray outward like a fan. They grow continuously from early spring to late fall. New growth is simply pulled off gently with the fingertips as it is determined that growth in the area is not wanted or needed. For areas that need to be filled in, simply allow adjacent growth to occupy this area by leaving it untouched. This group is perhaps the easiest type of bonsai to prune. New growth can easily be pulled off with the fingertips. Older growth that does not pull off must be pruned off with pruning shears, and if this is a necessity, it means you waited too long between prunings. Regular pruning every week for plants of this group insures that your tree will always be growing in the proper direction and will not have brown areas of growth at any time during the year.

Fig. 11-8. This juniper is just starting to extend its growth in spring. Gently pull off the tips that are still chartreuse.

Fig. 11-9. Tender shoots of cryptomeria are left alone. If pruning is necessary, use sharp pointed shears to remove clumps of unwanted growth after it has hardened off.

The Fir Group

These trees include the false fir, the true fir, hemlock, spruce, and larch. It is recognized that larch is in fact a deciduous conifer, but it should be treated as a member of this group for purposes of pruning. Its growth characteristics are very close to the fir, spruce, and hemlock, and these methods should be applied. Other deciduous conifers that should be included with this group are the bald cypress, Montezuma cypress, dawn redwood, and tamarack. The needle growth of this group of trees is characterized by rows of needles along each small branchlet. Sometimes the needles appear only to the right and left of each branchlet; sometimes they appear to the right and left as well as top needles, as in the fir and spruce. The one thing this group has in common is the array of latent buds appearing along the branches. In most trees, these latent buds are simply too small to see. In such trees as the Douglas fir and the western larch, these buds are large enough so that you can actually direct growth. But in most cases, they are too small to see. They do not appear at the base of each needle, but they appear every half-inch (1.7 cm), or inch (2.5 cm) along new growth. These latent buds remain as potential buds as long as there is not a great deal of bark on the branch. As branches age, these latent buds will disappear.

Fig. 11-11. This fir is at the perfect stage to remove the young tips. This will cause back-budding and shorter internodes.

Fig. 11-12. Spruce must have its top leaders totally removed to compact this strong upright grower.

Fig. 11-10. This cypress has golden, tender new growth. Pull off this growth to compact your bonsai. Allow it to extend for a weeping effect.

The proper procedure for pruning this group is to remove all new growth as it appears in early spring. New growth will appear as a slight, very tight ball of chartreuse needles all clustered together. This is a more rounded shape than the pine candle and can be easily pulled off the tree when it is young and succulent. After this new growth is pulled off, latent buds behind these buds along the branch will become activated and will begin to grow. At the tip of the branch where you just pruned, news buds will also appear.

Fig. 11-13. Latent buds on larch are just barely visible to the eye. Prune for shape, and then in a few weeks prune for bud location and direction after buds show themselves.

This pruning technique causes a large surge in growth all along the branch as well as on the tips of the branch and it becomes the task of the bonsai grower to select the growth that is to be saved and to remove the growth which is not needed. Again, pruning in a timely fashion is important on trees of this type. If you wait too long, growth will harden off and become a dark green color, and you will need to use pruning shears rather than your fingertips. If you are able to always use your finger-

tips on this type of bonsai plant, it means that you are pruning in a timely fashion.

Fig. 11-14. For weeping varieties such as hemlock, allow some new shoots to extend themselves to full length. Thin the branches to allow even distribution of sun to the interior foliage.

TRAINING TECHNIQUES

The previous chapter discussed the pinch-and-grow technique known to the Chinese as *lingnan*. This chapter discusses some of the more recent advances in bonsai technology. Bonsai pruning purists will be attracted to the older Chinese style, whereas those who appreciate advanced trained techniques will appreciate this chapter. It is merely a matter of personal taste.

WIRING

The purpose of wiring a branch is fairly straightforward and is a concept that is easy to understand. If a branch is in the incorrect position, it is possible to wind wire around it and secure it into a position that is more favorable or desired by the designer. Most wire used in bonsai is annealed copper wire.

Fig. 12-1. This elm is being bent by use of a bonsai clamp.

Copper has many positive attributes. Copper is a poison, but when used in small, controlled quantities on bonsai, it contributes to the dwarfing of the foliage. Each time the bonsai is watered, a bit of copper oxide comes off the training wire and is deposited in the soil. This contributes to the dwarfing of the plant.

Annealed copper wire between the sizes of 24-gauge and 4-gauge is the most common size for bonsai training. For copper wiring, one selects a wire that is about one-third the diameter of the branch to be trained. The wire is secured along the trunk for at least three turns and then is coiled around the branch for its entire length. Excess wire is trimmed off with wire cutters and the branch can be bent into the desired position. After a period of about a year, the wire can be cut off and the branch will remain in its new trained position. Far more common in the bonsai marketplace is copper-clad aluminum wire. This is aluminum wire that has been coated with a copper-colored plating. It is far more

accessible and is easier to bend. This aluminum wire is available in millimeter diameters from one millimeter to six millimeters. The correct size of aluminum wire to select for bending a branch is about half the size of the branch diameter. The reason this is different from copper wire is that aluminum is softer and easier to bend.

To bend a young trunk, the same principles apply, except that instead of securing the wire on the trunk as previously described, the wire is secured in the soil. Simply plunge the end of the wire into the soil between the roots somewhere near the back of the root buttress. The wire should plunge deep, clear to the bottom of the container, and then the wire is coiled around loosely to the top of the trunk. Use an even, 45-degree angle, similar to what you might see on a barber pole. At no time should a wire be applied snugly to a branch or trunk because this does not allow for future growth of the branch or trunk. Wire that is too tight will

Fig. 12-2. When fastening a live branch to a dead jin, *be sure to protect the live bark with a small twig.*

Fig. 12-3. Always wire loosely to allow for next year's growth.

scar the trunk or branch. Make sure there is plenty of air space between the applied wire and the living plant tissue. As you come to the tip of a branch or the apex of a trunk, you will find that the wire becomes more difficult to wind. Use small needle-nose pliers to assist you in finishing the wires at this point. If you wish to change your wire or have incorrectly wired for any reason, be sure to cut off your wire. Do not attempt to unwind the wire, or damage to the bark and the sensitive cambium layer below will result. To cut off wire, you will need a wire cutter that cuts on the tips of the jaws. There are wire cutters available that have the ability to cut wire close to the joint or rivet of the tool. These are not appropriate tools for bonsai purposes, because you can not trim off wire from a branch. The type of wire cutter that is able to cut wire at the very tip is the type that you will need.

Fig. 12-5. Bend a forward-facing branch upwards to make a new, lower apex. Protect all live bark with a small twig.

BENDING LARGER BRANCHES

Fig. 12-4 shows the silhouette of a large alpine branch that has experienced a great deal of snow load every winter. To reproduce this type of effect on bonsai, bend branches down. With some imagination, some simple hardware, and a bit of engineering, it's possible to design ways to draw down large branches on older nursery stock.

One method that works well for me is to use wire to pull branches down directly toward the pot. Instead of securing the wire around the trunk and then coiling it out onto the branch, secure the wire directly around the branch about halfway from the trunk to the tip of the branch. Protect this connection. Unprotected wire looped around a branch will scar it in only a few days. Place some cork or a small twig around the branch where you are going to secure one end of your wire. This will keep the wire from cutting into the bark of your branch. The other end of the branch can be fastened to the pot or a root down below.

Sometimes where no fastening is available, an additional coil of wire around the pot will provide a place to fasten the other end of your first wire. By drawing down the branch carefully with one hand, you can secure the other end of your wire with the other hand. After about one year, the wire can be cut and the branch will remain approximately in the position where you have moved it. When wiring branches, always move your branches a little bit farther than you think is nec-

Fig. 12-4.

essary. Often when the wire is cut off, the branch will try to restore its original shape. If you overcompensate slightly with your training, the branch will return to a position that is more to your liking.

Turnbuckles are another way to influence the direction of large branches. By fastening one end of the turnbuckle to the branch and the other end to a secure setting, the turnbuckle can be moved a bit every day, thereby moving a fairly large branch. It is suprising how powerful the strength of the screw

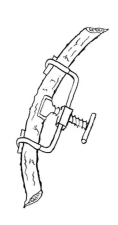

Fig. 12-6.

is on a turnbuckle. Once the turnbuckle is in place, you can turn it slightly every day until the branch is in the position which is desired. By adding a few extra turns over the course of the next few months, you can intentionally overcompensate for the direction of the branch, to assure yourself that when the turnbuckle is moved, it will not spring back into its original position. With the great forces involved, make extra sure live plant tissue is always well padded and protected from damage.

Manufactured bonsai clamps are available to the avid bonsai grower. These are devices that are designed to bend large branches. They consist of two hooks with a screw-type piston halfway between. It is possible to put one of these training devices on a fairly large trunk or branch and move it an incredible distance over time in a safe fashion. It is an ingenious device, similar to having three turnbuckles attached to the same branch. Imagine one turnbuckle pulling on a branch, while two adjacent turnbuckles are pulling in the opposite direction. Over time, one can accomplish large bends in fairly large diameter branches and trunks.

Delaminating a branch is yet another technique for bending large-diameter material. It should only be used in special situations where extremely large branches must be moved or the basic design of the tree will be lost. There is a special tool called a bonsai delaminater, sometimes known as a branch splitter. It is employed in a horizontal fashion on the branch. The branch is split lengthwise. Once the branch has been split, it will bend more easily, because it is easier to bend two smaller pieces of branch than it is to bend one large branch. This method should only be used for rapidly growing trees because the scar that results is noticeable. On slower-growing species, the scar will remain for too many years for this method to have any practical value.

REMOVING LARGE BRANCHES

Sometimes it is necessary to cut off a very large branch in order to achieve your bonsai design. There are two ways of doing this so that it looks natural. The first method is to try to hide the scar by hollowing it out. The second method is to pretend that nature meant to have the scar highly visible and it is actually carved and made to be an important part of the total bonsai design.

The Jin

The second-most useful way to remove large branches from bonsai material is to carve or shape the branch into a dead remnant such as is found in nature. Copying some of the interesting and picturesque *jin* and *shari* found at high altitudes or at the beach can add interest to a tree that it might lack if the scar were merely hollowed out. For this type of technique, though, it must be stressed that the deadwood is preserved. An application of lime sulfur is

Fig. 12-8. To keep this jin preserved, coat it with lime sulfur every summer.

Fig. 12-7. Jin, shari, and saba miki make secure and safe attachments for training wire.

important to the preservation of these dead elements on a tree. At high altitude, the drying winds and the high amount of ultraviolet light will help to preserve these parts. In lower-altitude bonsai application, these sections of deadwood will turn black, get soft, and drop off. Once they drop off, a soft scar remains that still needs preservation or it will continue to rot the rest of the tree. Such areas must be protected with some kind of wood preservative. An annual application of lime sulfur, full-strength, seems to be the best solution to preserve deadwood. Not only does it prevent insects and disease from attacking this deadwood, but it imparts a beautiful silvery gray color that resembles driftwood.

Fig. 12-9 shows some nursery stock of a Japanese flowering cherry. The top of the plant has died away because of winter frost, but the bottom part is continuing to thrive. This plant makes excellent bonsai material, especially excellent material for miniature bonsai. The top of this tree must be cut off in order to reduce the height of this

105

Fig. 12-9.

plant, and to eliminate most of this original dead trunk. It's possible to carve the top of this tree to look like the tops of trees in alpine or desert areas. It's possible to artificially carve knot-holes and swirling wood grain so that this tree will look hundreds of years old even though it is only five years old. This deadwood then must be preserved with lime sulfur in order to keep it from turning black and rotting away. **Fig. 12-10** shows a fine example of a driftwood-style *saba miki*. This drift-wood is just starting to turn dark and is ready for its next application of lime sulfur. If this were allowed to go un-touched for yet one more year, the color

Fig. 12-10.

would be even darker, the wood would start to soften, and the total bonsai would be lost. These areas must be protected.

ROOT PRUNING

Tools

It is possible to use regular bonsai pruning tools inside the root ball to cut roots, but it is not highly recom-mended. Most bonsai soil or potting soil or any kind, contains a certain amount of inorganic material. This material may be sand, mica, ver-miculite, decomposed granite, or lava cinders. It is very damaging to any shears or bonsai scissors to try to cut roots growing in any of these mineral, granular soil components. Sometimes it is necessary to use these tools, how-ever, and I offer the following compro-mise. Before trimming roots on a bon-sai, wash them with a sharp blast of water from a spray bottle. This will usually dislodge any granules that may

Fig. 12-11. Sometimes roots make a convenient and safe attachment for vertical training wires.

be getting in the way of your pruning shears. Also, it is possible to avoid damage to your shears simply by cutting slowly. Sharp, quick cuts inside the soil ball will usually damage the shears, but if you slowly press the handles of your shears together and allow time for sand or grit to move out of the way, it is possible to safely trim roots with standard bonsai shears.

For most root pruning, however, I find it far preferable to use a freezer saw or a serrated carving knife. These tools are easily sharpened. They are fairly inexpensive to purchase, and if damaged are very easy to replace. The main advantage of using these tools is that there are not two metal blades coming in contact with one another in order to sever a root. All you have is one serrated blade which basically saws through the soil and the roots simultaneously. Another device that works well for me for larger work is a small shingling hatchet. Unlike a common hatchet, this is a hatchet that has a bit longer blade and is a little narrower. It is used for splitting cedar shingles or shakes. It will penetrate easily and safely into a root ball without damaging the cutting edge of your bonsai shears.

Timing

For the health of the plant, it is preferable to do root pruning when the sap is flowing, but flowing slowly. We have

Fig. 12-13. Where there are bare spots in your design, consider grafting on a branch.

two windows of opportunity for extensive root pruning. These are in early spring and mid-fall. In early spring, as the temperature rises outside, the sap begins to flow within the tree. Nights are still cold and so there is not a great deal of sap pressure within the plant. Extensive root pruning may be done at this time by bare-rooting the plant with hard water pressure from a garden hose. The water is forceful and yet it gently dislodges all soil particles from the plant. The roots can be easily seen and safely pruned with normal bonsai shears. Earlier in the year, the sap is not moving and damaged roots are unable to protect themselves from insects and disease. In winter, root pruning is not advisable. Later in the spring, the sap has a very high pressure. It is at the highest pressure it will have all year long, and extensive root pruning will lead to excessive bleeding of the sap in the area of the root ball. This weakens the plant and leads to poor or no new growth in the top foliage. In the summer, the plant is too hot to root-prune.

The second window of opportunity for root pruning is in mid-fall just as the temperatures start to cool, where there is enough sap moving so that damaged areas can heal. Progressing toward winter, colder and colder temperatures make it impossible to do any further root pruning. At all times with root pruning, it is important to respect the life of the plant. Some untouched

Fig. 12-12. Exposed roots should be larger than a chopstick in diameter or they will dry out.

Fig. 12-14. Protect small live branches from summer heat. These will easily become sunburned and will crack and dry out.

Fig. 12-16. Strive for maximum secondary branch ramification. Pinch back new growth often.

Fig. 12-15. Carve saba miki to look like venerable old trees in the wilderness. Practice sculpting skills on pieces of driftwood from the beach.

white root hairs must remain on the root ball at all times. At no time is it appropriate to remove all the tips of all roots simultaneously, for then the tree will find it difficult to recover. Ideally, the amount of soil in your container should be around 50 percent in volume, the other 50 percent being the volume of the roots contained. As the bonsai gradually becomes root-bound, the root percentage will increase to 60 percent or possibly 70 percent of total volume. At this point, it is imperative that the plant be root-pruned in order to restore the 50/50 balance. If the root percentage becomes too high, it is difficult to uncoil the roots and to straighten them out without permanent, fatal damage to the tree. Regular pruning of the roots is as necessary as regular pruning of the branches. Once you allow yourself to get behind in your schedule, sometimes it is difficult to recover. After root pruning, a bit of immediate and judicious care is necessary to insure the life of your bonsai. Transfer the plant to a shady area and water it immediately. If your water contains a bit of vitamin B-1, it seems to recover more quickly. Small amounts of fertilizer may be added after a few days. Large amounts of fertilizer are inappropriate immediately after root pruning. Water the plant several times a day until it is obvious that the plant is doing well, and then move it slowly into the sun, first giving it only dappled sunlight for a few hours every day until it is finally back into a location appropriate to the species.

Fig. 12-17.

INDEX